Gofors & G

An A-Z of Bible characters l

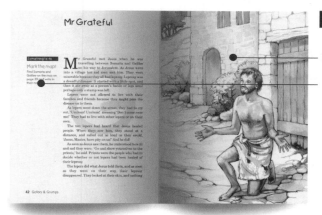

Mr Grateful

M r Grateful met Jesus when he was travelling between Samaria and Galilee on his way to Jerusalem. As Jesus went into a village ten sad men met him. They were miserable because they all had leprosy. Leprosy was a dreadful disease. It started with a little spot, and then it ate away as a person's hands or legs until perhaps only a stump was left.

Lepers were not allowed to live with their families and friends because they might pass the disease on to them.

As lepers went down the street, they had to cry out, 'Unclean! Unclean!' meaning 'Don't come near me!' They had to live with other lepers on their own.

The ten lepers had heard that Jesus healed people. When they saw him, they stood at a distance, and called out as loud as they could, 'Jesus, Master, have pity on us!' And he did!

As soon as Jesus saw them, he understood how ill and they were. 'Go and show yourselves to the priests,' he said. Priests were the people who had to decide whether or not lepers had been healed of their leprosy.

The lepers did what Jesus told them, and as soon as they went on their way, their leprosy disappeared. They looked at their skin, and nothing

Something to do
Mark the map!
Find Samaria and Galilee on the map on page 39 ... write in their ...

42 Gofors & Grumps

What's inside?

Illustrated throughout

Things to do

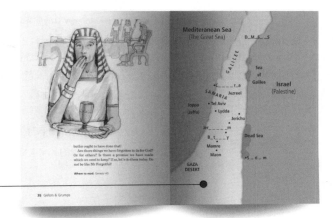

butler ought to have done that!
Are there things we have forgotten to do for God?
Or for others? Is there a promise we have made
which we need to keep? If so, let's do them today. Do
not be like Mr Forgetful!

Where to read: Genesis 40

38 Gofors & Grumps

Mediteranean Sea
(The Great Sea)   D_M_s..._s

GALILEE

Sea
of
Galilee   Israel
(Palestine)

...._r_a
SAMARIA   Jezreel
Joppa   • Tel Aviv
(Jaffa)   • Lydda
• Jericho
Jer...._m
B_t_._y   Dead Sea
Mamre
Maon   •s_6_m

GAZA
DESERT

Maps and puzzles

DayOne

© Derek Prime 2006

Originally published in 1995 as four separate volumes

ISBN 190308797-X

9 781903 087978

All Scripture quotations, unless otherwise indicated, are taken from
the **New International Version**®. Copyright © 1979 Hodder and Stoughton
Used by permission. All rights reserved.

British Library Cataloguing in Publication Data available

Published by Day One Publications
Ryelands Road, Leominster, HR6 8NZ
☎ 01568 613 740 FAX 01568 611 473
email—sales@dayone.co.uk
web site—www.dayone.co.uk
North American—email—sales@dayonebookstore.com
North American—web site—www.dayonebookstore.com

All rights reserved

No part of this publication may be reproduced, or stored in a retrieval system, or
transmitted, in any form or by any means, mechanical, electronic, photocopying,
recording or otherwise, without the prior permission of Day One Publications.

Designed by Steve Devane, illustrated by Ruth Goodridge
and printed by Gutenberg Press, Malta

Contents

Mr Afraid

The Scripture Union

The Scripture Union is an international, youth and Bible-reading movement. It works in more than seventy countries. It produces notes to help people of all ages to understand the Bible. The Bible Reading notes are used by more than one million readers. It arranges camps, beach missions and house parties for children and young people.

Are you ever afraid? I have often been afraid. And it still happens to me! In cartoons and story-books when people are afraid their knees knock or their teeth chatter. But usually when we are afraid we feel funny in our stomachs and our lips go dry.

Some of our fears are silly, but they are still real to us. Joseph Spiers was a man who encouraged people to read the Bible everyday, and he was the founder of the Scripture Union. But he had one special fear—he was afraid of cats!

One day a dreadful thing happened. He was visiting a home in which one of the children misbehaved. The boy was told by his parents to leave the room. The family then began to pray together. Suddenly the door opened, and the boy threw a cat into the room, and it landed on poor Mr Spiers's shoulders. With a terrified shriek he jumped up, ran out of the house and never came back again!

We may laugh at his fear of cats, but we can have fears that are just as silly.

I want to tell you about Mr Afraid. There are several people in the Bible who could be given that name, but we are going to think about the very first one.

His name was Adam, and he said 'I was afraid …

Did you know?

The Bible

The Bible is the world's best-selling book. The word 'Bible' comes from a Greek word meaning 'books', and the Bible contains 66 books. It is different from any other book because although lots of different people—probably as many as forty—wrote it, God made them want to write and helped them so that all they wrote is true.

Satan

Satan is another name for the devil. He is against all that is good, and he is behind everything that is evil in the world. He brought men and women under his power by tempting Adam and Eve to disobey God so that they and we deserve to die and to be separated from God.

The Bible does not explain why God allowed Satan to have such power, but it tells us the good news that the Lord Jesus came into the world as a human being so that he could break Satan's power: the Lord Jesus did this when he died on the Cross as a Substitute for sinners, and then rose again.

When the Lord Jesus returns, all Satan's power will be taken away from him for ever.

so I hid.' It all happened like this. When God made the world there was no fear anywhere. Everything God had made was perfect, so that he could say when he had finished, 'It is very good!'

The Bible tells us that Adam was the first man, and Eve the first woman. It is very hard for us to imagine but in the beginning they had no need to be afraid of some of the things that we are afraid of, like animals or anything else that God had made. And most important of all, they were not afraid of God because they knew he was their Friend. God came and talked with them each day, and spent time with them. And how Adam and Eve enjoyed his friendship!

But then something dreadful happened! God's enemy—Satan—tempted Adam and Eve to doubt God's love for them.

God had put Adam into the Garden of Eden to

take care of it. God said to Adam, 'You are free to eat from any tree in the garden, but you must not eat from the tree of the knowledge of good and evil. If you do, you will die.'

Not long after that Satan came along and said to Eve, 'Did God really say, "You must not eat from any tree in the garden"?' Satan then told Eve a lie. 'That's not true. You will not die. God said that because he knows that when you eat of it you will be like him and you will know what is good and what is bad.' Eve listened to Satan, and she took some of the fruit and ate it. She then gave some to Adam, and he ate it too.

They both disobeyed God. Can you guess one of the first things that happened? Yes, they were afraid!

That evening God came to talk to Adam and Eve as usual, and for the first time ever Adam tried to hide from God. He hid among the trees of the garden, or at least he thought he did, because no one can really hide from God.

God called to Adam, 'Where are you?' Adam answered, 'I heard you in the garden, and I was afraid, so I hid.'

Have you ever tried to hide because you have been afraid? Perhaps it was when you were small and naughty, and you tried to hide under a table or under your bed!

If we do something wrong, we may try to keep out of our parents' or teachers' way because we are afraid of what they will say or do.

Adam became the first Mr Afraid. With Eve his wife, they were Mr and Mrs Afraid. And ever since all the members of their family—and that includes us—have been born afraid.

Our Bible dictionary

Death

Death first came into the world when Adam and Eve disobeyed God and rebelled against him. They immediately lost their friendship with God which was a kind of death inside them—a spiritual death—and then later their bodies died. Death has spread to everyone because we have all disobeyed God and sinned. By dying in the place of sinners, the Lord Jesus died the death we deserve. When we trust in him, we do not have to be afraid of death because he gives us eternal life. In heaven there will be no more death.

The Cross

The Cross is a word used to describe the painful death the Lord Jesus suffered when he was nailed to a wooden stake or beam. Because he died in the place of sinners, as their Substitute, the Cross sums up the wonderful good news that the Lord Jesus died for our sins that we might be forgiven.

Did you know?

Hymns

A 'hymn' is another word for a song. But it is a word especially kept for songs that praise God.

Can you remember what it was that Adam did which brought fear into the world and made him Mr Afraid? It was his disobeying God, and disobeying God is sin.

You and I were born Master or Miss Afraid, and we grow up to be Mr and Mrs Afraid because we too disobey God.

Can we stop being Master or Miss Afraid? Yes, we can, because the Lord Jesus, God's Son, came to take away our fears. That is good news for everyone.

The most wonderful thing the Lord Jesus did was to die for us on the Cross. He died as our Substitute. Do you know what a substitute is? We have substitutes in games like football and rugby, and in athletics. A substitute takes someone else's place. We deserve to be punished for our sins. But the Lord Jesus, who never did wrong, took our place and accepted our punishment so that we might be forgiven. A popular hymn puts it well—

He died that we might be forgiven,
He died to make us good,
That we might go at last to heaven,
Saved by his precious blood.

There was no other good enough
To pay the price of sin;
He only could unlock the gate
Of heaven, and let us in.

When we trust the Lord Jesus as our Saviour, he promises to be with us always. When I was a little boy I was sometimes afraid at night, and my mother or father would come into my bedroom and stay by me until I went to sleep. Did that happen to you?

Because we know our parents love us, our fears go away when they are near us.

My fears disappear when I remember that the Lord Jesus promises never to leave me. When we trust him as our Saviour, his Spirit lives in us, and he helps us overcome our fears.

There is a song which says,

Trust and obey,
for there's no other way
to be happy in Jesus,
but to trust and obey.

I like the story of the small boy at Sunday School who had misunderstood the words, and he was singing, 'Trust and OK!' But he was right! When Mr Afraid trusts in the Lord Jesus, his fears are overcome, and he is OK!

Where to read: Genesis 3:1–21

Something to do:

Can you think of things of which you are afraid or about which you get worried?

See what God says in the Bible we should do about:
our fears—Psalm 56:3
our anxieties—
Philippians 4:6–7

Jerusalem

Jerusalem is one of the oldest cities in the world. King David made it his capital city, and his son Solomon built God's House— the Temple—there. It is very high up in the hills, and the ground slopes away steeply on three of its sides. That is why people are said to 'go up' to Jerusalem or 'down' from it. The Lord Jesus was often in Jerusalem, and it was outside the walls of the city that he was put to death.

Miss Busy

Are you sometimes busy? I want to tell you about Miss Busy. Her real name was Martha, and she was a friend of Jesus. She lived in a village called Bethany, which was not far from Jerusalem, the capital city of Israel. She had a sister, called Mary, who was probably younger than she was.

Whenever Jesus went to Jerusalem, he would call in and see the two sisters and their brother Lazarus, and sometimes stay with them.

One day Jesus arrived in Bethany with his disciples and Martha and Mary were so glad to see them all again. They welcomed them into their home.

Immediately Martha thought, 'What am I going

A disciple

A disciple is someone who wants to be taught by a teacher, and so it was a good name for the first followers of the Lord Jesus, and for all today who follow him. His disciples are those who trust him as their Saviour and live as he tells them to do. A disciple is another name for a Christian.

to cook for them to eat?' And she got all in a fluster about it.

But her sister Mary did not think first about food. Instead she wanted to listen to Jesus, because she knew that no one else spoke or taught like him.

As Jesus' disciples sat round him, Mary sat on the floor listening to him too. She took notice of everything that he said. She knew she was learning important things about God and how to trust and please him.

But Martha thought she did not have time to sit down and listen. 'Jesus is a very special guest,' she thought to herself. 'I must get him and the disciples the best meal possible. Now what meat is there in the larder? Have I enough vegetables? And what shall I give them to eat as a sweet?' She began to think of all the things she had to get ready.

What happens in your home when visitors come? Do you eat in the dining room instead of in the kitchen? Does your mother put out the best tablecloth and serviettes, and perhaps the best china and knives and forks? That is the kind of thing Martha did.

As she began to get things organised, she thought, 'Where's Mary? She ought to be helping me. They are her guests as much as mine.'

She peeped into the room where Jesus and his disciples were, and there was Mary sitting on the floor listening to Jesus. Martha tried to attract her attention, but Mary did not see her because she was listening so carefully to Jesus.

Back went Martha to the kitchen, feeling all hot and bothered. The more she thought of Mary sitting with Jesus, the bigger the clatter I think she made with the pots and pans.

As Martha cooked the meal she became hotter and hotter, and her hair more and more untidy. Everything seemed to go wrong. Pots boiled over, and she did not have enough hands for all she had to do!

She poked her head into the room again to catch Mary's eye, but she did not succeed. In the end she could stand it no longer. She marched into the

Something to do

Mark the map!

Find where the country of Israel, the city of Jerusalem, and the village of Bethany are on the map on page 39 and write in their names.

room, went up to Jesus, and said, 'Lord, don't you care that my sister has left me to do all the work by myself. Tell her to come and help me.'

Jesus knew all that Martha was thinking. He looked at her and said, 'Martha, Martha! You are worried and upset about many things. But really there is only one thing you ought to be concerned about. Mary has discovered it, and I won't take it away from her.'

Poor Miss Busy! She had not realised that the most important thing to do for Jesus was not just to feed him but to give him her time.

Martha had done the right thing in opening her home to Jesus. But she made so much fuss about the little details that she had no time left simply to be with him. He had not come just to eat, but to see her and Mary.

We can be like Miss Busy. If we give our time to the wrong things, we may forget to give time to people. When guests come to our home, we may be too busy playing or watching television to talk to them.

Parents can sometimes be too busy to give time to their children. A father's work took him away from home, and as he thought about his wife and children, he felt sorry he had been too busy to spend time with them. He decided that when he arrived home, he would buy them all presents. That was kind, but much more important than presents was his being with his family and doing things with them.

The Lord Jesus wants us to think of other people. He does not want us to be so busy that we do not have time for those who need our help.

We can even be too busy to give time to the Lord

Jesus. If we trust him as our Saviour, he wants us to get to know him better—just as he wanted Martha to know him better. We do that by talking to him in prayer and by reading his Word, the Bible.

If we leave it until late in the evening, we may become too tired. And if we do not get up early enough in the morning, we may not have time. Never get so tired or so busy that you do not have time to give to the Lord Jesus.

Miss Busy has a lesson to teach us. More important than all the things we may do for Jesus is our listening to him as we read the Bible, and our talking to him when we pray.

Where to read: Luke 10:38–42

Choices

Can you make a list of five things about which you have to make choices? Let me give you one with which to start

1. Clothes to wear.

2.

3.

4.

5.

Mr Choose-for-myself

There are some things we do most days of the week. One is making choices. We choose our friends at school. We choose which games or toys we are going to play with, or which books we are going to read.

Perhaps on special occasions we go to a restaurant, and we have to choose from a menu what we would like to eat. When a plate of cakes is offered us, we have to choose which one we want.

Something to do

Mark the map!

Find where Ur is on the map on page 41 and write in its name.

Can you draw?

Draw two roads, one wide with lots of people on it, and the other narrow with few people on it. Put a signpost on each showing to where the roads lead. Then write underneath the Lord Jesus's words in Matthew 7:13–14.

Have you ever had an argument when someone has taken the cake you would have chosen? But there are much more important choices than these! Do you remember the story of Miss Busy—Martha—and her sister Mary? Which one made the right choice when Jesus came to their home?

The Lord Jesus spoke about the most important choice of all—the choice of which road we are going to take in life. He said, 'Enter through the narrow gate. For wide is the gate and broad is the road that leads to destruction, and many enter through it. But small is the gate and narrow the road that leads to life, and only a few find it.'

Jesus tells us that most people make the wrong choice when they choose how to spend their lives.

The problem is that so often we want to choose for ourselves, and we do not listen to what God says.

Let me tell you about Mr Choose-for-myself. His real name was Lot.

Lot had a kind uncle whose name was Abraham. Abraham lived for many years in a city called Ur. But one day God told Abraham to move, and to go to a place that he was going to show him. Lot went too, and he took his wife and family with him.

Abraham was wealthy and owned lots of sheep, goats, silver and gold. At first Abraham's family and servants and Lot's stayed close to one another. They lived in tents in the hills where there was plenty of grass for their cattle to eat.

But one day there was a quarrel. The men who looked after Abraham's cattle wanted to move the animals to a place where the grass was greener. But the men who looked after Lot's cattle wanted to go to the same place, and so they quarrelled.

Abraham made a good suggestion to Lot. 'Don't

let's have any quarrelling between you and me, or between your men and mine, for we are members of the same family. Isn't the whole land before us? Let's move away from one another. If you go to the left, I'll go to the right; if you go to the right, then I'll go to the left.'

That was generous of Abraham. Let's imagine a boy opens a box of chocolates, and his grandmother and sister are with him. Who should have first choice? And who should have second? Who should be last?

Think now of Abraham and Lot, his nephew. Who should have had first choice? Yes, Abraham, but he did not want a fuss, and he certainly did not want Lot to be resentful. Abraham, as Lot's uncle, could have said, 'I'll take this land, and you go over there.' But he did not.

When Abraham gave Lot first choice, Lot could have said, 'No, uncle, you choose first.' But sadly he did not.

Lot stood and looked at all the land he could see around him. He looked one way and saw that the grass was dry. His cattle would not grow very fat there. He looked the other way. That was much better! The grass was green, and there were trees, and a river.

Lot thought, 'That's the better land. I'll go there.'

But Lot made a big mistake. He did not stop to ask for God's help in the choice he made, and he did not think which choice God might prefer him to make.

God would probably have said to him, 'Let Abraham choose first—don't be selfish.'

God would certainly have said, 'Lot, that land is

Did you know?

Ur

Ur was a famous city, on the river Euphrates, in southern Babylonia (modern Iraq). It was the family home of Abraham. It was finally abandoned as a city about 300 BC, and it had been lived in for several thousands of years before that. The ruins of a great temple tower with lots of steps (called a ziggurat) still remain, and lots of interesting things have been found by archaeologists as they have dug in the ground.

Something to do

Mark the map!

It is not easy for us to mark Sodom on our map because where it probably was now lies submerged in the Dead Sea. Find the Dead Sea on page 39 and put in the city of Sodom at its southern end.

near a wicked city, and living there will be dangerous for you and your family.'

The Bible says that Lot 'chose for himself the whole plain of the Jordan and set out towards the east'.

In choosing for himself, Lot chose selfishly. He was not thinking 'God first' or 'Others first' but 'Me first'. That is what we call selfishness.

If we saw two parcels containing presents, one with attractive wrapping paper and the other with ordinary brown paper, and we were told we could choose one of them, I expect we would choose the one with the attractive wrapping paper. But that might not be the better choice! What looks attractive may not always be the best. Lot was

foolish enough to be guided only by what his eyes saw.

In choosing for himself, Lot put himself into bad company. He pitched his tents near Sodom, a dangerous and evil place. At first Lot lived near Sodom, and then he lived in the city itself. Later on he had to be rescued, first by Abraham and then by two angels. Sodom was then destroyed and Lot's wife died—and all because Lot was Mr Choose-for-myself.

Abraham was quite different! We may call him Mr Let-God-choose-for-me! And he was rewarded. After Lot made his choice, and left Abraham, the Lord said to Abraham, 'Lift up your eyes from where you are and look north and south, east and west. All the land that you see I will give you and your family for ever.' When we want to choose what pleases God, we always receive his best.

We are all like either Lot or Abraham. We are either people who simply choose for ourselves or those who want to choose what God says is best for us.

The Lord Jesus died that we might be forgiven for being people who choose only for themselves, and instead become people who want to choose what God wants.

If the Lord Jesus is our Saviour, we can pray to him about our choices, and he will help us make the right ones.

Where to read: Genesis 13:1–18

Mr Doubter

Did you know?

Crucifixion

Crucifixion was a punishment the Romans used. It was a cruel way to make people die. A person first lay on the ground, and his hands were nailed to the main crossbar. Then the crossbar was lifted up by ropes and fixed to an upright stake. It was such a horrible punishment that the Romans never used it for their own people but only for slaves and rebellious people whom they had conquered.

D
o you know what a doubter is? A doubter is someone who does not believe what he is told or is not sure if something is true. If you climbed up a tree, and then could not get down, and your friends said 'Jump, and we'll catch you' you might doubt if they could! We sometimes doubt because we are afraid, or because we do not trust what people say.

Thomas was Mr Doubter. He and all the other disciples and friends of Jesus were very upset when Jesus died on the Cross. Although Jesus had told them that it was going to happen, and that he was going to rise again, they had not really understood what he said to them.

Jesus was crucified on a Friday, and on the Sunday afterwards the disciples heard amazing news: Jesus is alive! First, women had gone to the

Lord

Besides being the ordinary word to describe a person's boss or a slave's master, the word 'Lord' is a special name kept for God alone in the Bible. 'Lord' was the name or title the first followers of Jesus used when they spoke to him or about him. When we say 'Jesus is Lord' we are saying that he is God, and that he is worthy of our worship, service and obedience.

tomb early in the morning, and they had found it empty! Then Peter and John went to look, and they found it empty too.

But it was not only the empty grave that surprised them. Jesus then met and spoke to Mary, and also to two disciples walking home from Jerusalem.

That Sunday night the disciples were together. The doors were locked because they were afraid of the Jewish leaders who had been against Jesus. Suddenly Jesus came and stood among them, and he greeted them. He showed them his hands and his side. They could see with their own eyes the marks of the nails where he had been crucified, and where a soldier had thrust a spear into his side.

When they realised that it was true, that Jesus had really risen from the dead, and is alive, they were so glad! They were the happiest they had ever been in their lives! After talking to them for a little while, Jesus left them.

But one disciple was absent. It was Thomas. We do not know why he was not there. Perhaps he was too upset about Jesus' death to want to be with other people. Thomas loved the Lord Jesus very much. He once told the Lord Jesus that he was willing to die for him, and he really meant it.

When Thomas returned to the other disciples, the first thing they said to him was, 'We have seen the Lord!' They told him all Jesus had said to them, and how he had shown them his hands and his side.

But Thomas doubted! It was too good to be true. He did not think it could have happened. He knew Jesus had really died. He had seen what the soldiers did to Jesus as they nailed him to the Cross.

Thomas said to the other disciples, 'Unless I see

Satan

Satan is another name for the devil. He is against all that is good, and he is behind everything that is evil in the world. He brought men and women under his power by tempting Adam and Eve to disobey God so that they and we deserve to die and to be separated from God.

The Bible does not explain why God allowed Satan to have such power, but it tells us the good news that the Lord Jesus came into the world as a human being so that he could break Satan's power: the Lord Jesus did this when he died on the Cross as a Substitute for sinners, and then rose again.

When the Lord Jesus returns, all Satan's power will be taken away from him for ever.

the nail marks in his hands and put my finger where the nails were, and put my hand into his side, I will not believe it.'

He loved the Lord Jesus so much that he could not bear the thought of the disciples being wrong in what they said. He needed to see for himself.

Thomas must have spent a miserable week! I expect the other disciples kept on telling him to believe, and that made it all the more difficult for him.

But then the following Sunday something wonderful happened! The disciples were all together again in the house, and this time Thomas was there. Although the doors were locked, Jesus came and stood among them, and said, 'Peace be with you!'

Then the Lord Jesus looked at Thomas, and said to him, 'Put your finger here; see my hands. Reach out your hand and put it into my side. Don't doubt any longer. Believe!'

Thomas did not need to touch the marks of the wounds. He knew that it was Jesus. All his doubts went, and he was now sure Jesus had really risen from the dead! Thomas answered, 'My Lord and my God!'

The Lord Jesus then said to him, 'Because you have seen me, you have believed; happy are those who believe without seeing me!' Jesus was talking then of people like us.

I am glad the Bible tells us about Thomas—Mr Doubter. Satan will often try to sow doubts in our minds about Jesus and about what God says to us in his Word, the Bible.

If doubts come, remember the Lord Jesus knows all about them. He does not stop loving us if doubts come to our minds, just as he did not stop loving Thomas when he had doubts.

Whatever doubts we have, we should tell the Lord Jesus about them as we pray. It will not be long then before they will disappear, just as Thomas's did.

The Lord Jesus loves to help us understand what is true, and he wants us to be sure that he is alive for ever.

Where to read: John 20:19–31

Mr Evangelist

Something to do

Mark the map!

Find where Caesarea and the Mediterranean Sea are on the map on page 39 and write in their names.

Do you know what an evangelist is? He is someone who tells others the good news about Jesus. The good news is that Jesus is the Son of God who died and rose again from the dead to bring us back to God.

If we look up the word 'evangel' in a dictionary it tells us that it means 'good news'. An evangelist is the name given to a person who shares the good news of Jesus with others.

Of course, God wants every Christian to share the good news about Jesus. But he gives special ability to some people to be evangelists. One of the first was Philip. He is called Philip the evangelist in the Bible in the Book of Acts and that helps us not to mix him up with another Philip who was one of the Lord Jesus' first followers.

We do not know a lot about him. Besides speaking Hebrew, the language of the Jews, he could also speak Greek. He was married and had at least four children. The four children we know about were all girls, and their family home was in Caesarea, a city in Israel, on the Mediterranean Sea.

The first time we hear about Philip in the Bible is when the Church began in Jerusalem.

The twelve apostles decided that seven men who were good examples of what it means to be a Christian should be put in charge of looking after

Our Bible dictionary

Apostles

An apostle is someone sent out as a messenger. Although it can mean any sort of messenger, it describes the men the Lord Jesus first chose to be his special followers so that they might be eye-witnesses of his life and work, and especially of his resurrection.

Our Bible dictionary

Persecute, Persecution

To persecute is to treat people cruelly and unfairly usually because of what they believe. From the beginning Christians have often been persecuted because of their faith. See what the Lord Jesus says in John 15:20–21. Persecution of Christians still happens in many parts of the world.

the Church's money so that widows, orphans and other needy people would be properly cared for. Philip was one of the seven men chosen.

Soon after that, Stephen, who was another one of the seven, was put to death because of his faith in the Lord Jesus. Men who did not want him to preach about the Lord Jesus threw large stones and rocks at him. Many Christians had to leave Jerusalem as the persecution increased, and Philip was one of them. He went to Samaria, and there he told lots of people the good news. Many believed in Jesus, and there was great joy in the city.

Philip was a faithful evangelist. He carefully explained how God tells us to repent of our sins and to believe in the Lord Jesus who died in our place as sinners and who then rose again. Philip shared God's wonderful promise that those who repent and believe in Jesus are forgiven their sins and become God's children.

One day while Philip was busy in Samaria, an angel of the Lord said to him, 'Get ready and go to the road that runs through the desert to Gaza.'

That must have seemed a strange place to go, but Philip obeyed. It was not long before he discovered why God wanted him there. Who should be coming along the road in a chariot but a very important man from Ethiopia!

Every country needs someone to look after its money, and to see that it is spent wisely. The man in the chariot did this for his country. He had been visiting Jerusalem, but now was on his way back to Ethiopia.

He had gone to Jerusalem to worship God. As he returned home in his chariot he was reading the book of Isaiah the prophet, which is part of the Bible. God's Spirit said to Philip, 'Go over to that chariot and walk beside it.'

Philip ran up to the chariot and listened to the man reading Isaiah. The Ethiopian probably read it aloud to help him understand what he read. What he read was not written in the Ethiopian language but in Greek.

Philip asked him, 'Do you understand what you are reading?'

'How can I?' he replied, 'unless someone explains it to me?' He invited Philip to climb up into the chariot so that he might explain it to him.

The Ethiopian had read up to the words in Isaiah which speak of Jesus' death, where Isaiah says, 'He was led like a sheep to the slaughter, and as a lamb before the shearer is silent, so he did not open his mouth.'

The Ethiopian asked Philip, 'Tell me, please, was the prophet talking about himself or someone else?'

Our Bible dictionary

Repentance

To repent is to be really sorry for wrong things we have done. But it means more than simply being sorry: it means stopping doing wrong things, and instead doing the good things that please God.

Prophet

A prophet was someone who received God's message for others, and then spoke it to them—and sometimes wrote it down. Sometimes the prophets said what was going to happen in the future, but the most important thing was that they always delivered God's message faithfully, whether it was about the past, the present or the future.

Something to do

Mark the map!

Find where Samaria, the Gaza Desert and Ethiopia are on the maps on pages 39 and 41 and write in their names.

Saviour

A Saviour is someone who delivers or saves people from danger. It is a name especially given to the Lord Jesus because he died and rose again to save—or rescue—us from our sins and the death our sins deserve. His name 'Jesus' means 'God is the Saviour'.

Baptism

To baptise is to dip or plunge into water. Some Christians go right under the water when they are baptised and others have water poured or sprinkled on them. It is a picture first of washing. When we understand that the Lord Jesus died for our sins and we are really sorry for them, and we ask him to forgive us, baptism is a picture and sign of our being made clean from our sins. It is also like a badge showing that we have now become members of God's family through believing in Jesus, and we are his followers.

So Philip began to tell him the good news about Jesus from that part of the Bible.

Philip explained that Isaiah was talking about the Lord Jesus dying for our sins to bring us back to God. As soon as the Ethiopian understood this, he wanted to put his trust in the Lord Jesus as his Saviour and Lord. Philip told him that the way we show we believe in the Lord Jesus is by obeying his command to be baptised.

As they travelled along the road, they came to a place where there was some water and the Ethiopian said, 'Look, here is water. Why shouldn't I be baptised?' And he ordered the chariot to stop, and he and Philip went down into the water and Philip baptised him.

The Ethiopian went home tremendously happy because now the Lord Jesus was his Saviour, and he belonged to him.

He probably became the first missionary—or evangelist—to Ethiopia! Important people like kings and queens, presidents and government ministers, need a Saviour just as much as anyone else.

Philip is a good example to us. First, he really cared about people. That was why he was chosen to look after the widows and orphans in Jerusalem. Second, he was obedient to God. Even though he was in a hot desert, he ran to the chariot when God told him to do so when he told him to help the Ethiopian.

Third, he used the Bible to tell the Ethiopian the good news about Jesus. The best way to help others to believe in the Lord Jesus is to explain from the Bible what it tells us about his love in dying for us on the Cross. No wonder God used Philip!

All who love the Lord Jesus want to tell others about him. We may begin just where we are with our friends and neighbours. But we cannot tell others properly about the Lord Jesus as Saviour until first we trust him ourselves.

Where to read: Acts 8:26–40

A missionary

The word 'missionary' means someone who is sent. The Lord Jesus' last command to his followers was that they should go into all the world and tell people the good news about him. Those who obey his command and leave their own country to go to people in other parts of the world are called missionaries.

Can you draw?

A picture of Philip running up to the chariot in which the Ethiopian was returning home. You may like to draw it as a cartoon story with Philip then sitting in the chariot, and afterwards baptising the Ethiopian.

Mr Forgetful

Something to do

Mark the map!

Find Egypt on the map on page 41 and write in its name.

Do you ever forget things? Have you ever forgotten something really important? Mr Forgetful is the name we may give to the butler (or cup-bearer) who was in prison in Egypt with Joseph. His job was to taste whatever the king, or Pharaoh as he was called, was about to drink. He did this to make sure it was not poisoned, so that the king could safely drink it.

Joseph was in prison, not because he had done anything wrong, but because he had tried to do what was right. Sometimes doing what is right may get us into trouble as much as doing what is wrong. He was put in prison because people told lies about him.

But God was with Joseph, and it was not long before the chief jailer put Joseph in charge of the day to day running of the prison.

One day two men who had worked for the king of Egypt arrived in the prison as prisoners. They were the king's butler (or cup-bearer) and baker.

After they had been in prison awhile these two men both had dreams on the same night.

When Joseph saw them the next morning, they looked miserable, and so he asked them, 'What's wrong with you today?'

'We have both had dreams' they answered, 'but there is no one to interpret or explain their meaning.'

Joseph replied, 'God is the only one who can really

help us to interpret our dreams. Tell me what you dreamt.'

So the butler said, 'In my dream I saw a vine in front of me, and on the vine were three branches. As soon as it budded, and its clusters ripened into grapes, Pharaoh's cup was in my hand, and I took the grapes, squeezed them into Pharaoh's cup and put the cup in his hand.'

'I know what the dream means,' Joseph told him. 'The three branches are three days. Within three days Pharaoh will give you back your job, and you will put Pharaoh's cup into his hand, just as you used to do.'

Did you know?

A vine

A vine is a climbing and trailing plant which bears grapes from which wine is made. The ground or field in which vines grow is a vineyard.

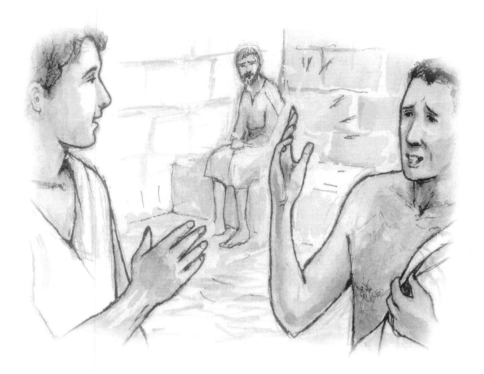

Then Joseph made a special request. 'When all goes well with you, please remember me, and mention me to Pharaoh, and ask him to release me from prison. I was kidnapped from the land of the Hebrews, and I have done nothing wrong to deserve being in prison.'

And, of course, the butler said 'yes'.

The chief baker then told Joseph his dream. 'I too had a dream. On my head were three baskets of bread. In the top basket were all kinds of baked goods for Pharaoh, but the birds came and ate them.'

Joseph looked sad. 'This is what it means. Three days from now Pharaoh will lift off your head and hang you on a tree, and birds will come and eat your body.'

Three days later was Pharaoh's birthday and he gave a party for all his officials. He gave the butler back his job, but he sentenced the baker to death, just as Joseph had said.

Do you remember what Joseph had asked the chief butler to do for him? Yes, to mention him to Pharaoh and to ask for his release from prison. But the Bible says, 'The chief cup-bearer, however, did not remember Joseph; he forgot him.' He was Mr Forgetful!

Joseph had to spend two more years in prison. We are not told why the butler forgot him. Perhaps he was too excited about his own release from prison to remember his promise. There were so many things for him to do. He was busy enjoying being free.

Joseph waited in prison, not knowing that the butler had forgotten all about him.

We can be forgetful, can't we? We can forget God. Perhaps we sometimes spend a whole day—or even a week—without talking to him.

Can you draw?

Draw what the butler and the baker saw in their dreams.

We can be forgetful of others. Have you ever tucked into a box of sweets and forgotten that there were others who ought to have shared them?

We can forget our promises like the butler did. He probably really meant it when he said to Joseph, 'I won't forget you.' But he did. When we hear a missionary speak about his or her work, we may promise, 'I'll pray for you' and then forget.

We can forget God's Word too. We may read it or listen to it being taught, and then go away and forget what God has said to us.

But there was Someone who did not forget Joseph! God did not forget him, and God never forgets us. Even if now and again our parents forget us for a moment, God does not.

What do you do when you do not want to forget something? I may write myself a little note, or perhaps tie a knot in my handkerchief!

We all need reminders to help us remember important things. God gives us Sunday so that we will remember that he made us, and that he raised Jesus from the dead.

He gives Christians the Lord's Supper—or the Communion Service—so that they never forget how much they owe to the Lord Jesus for dying for them.

One way of not forgetting about people who are important to us is to write their names down in a small book so that we remember to pray for them every day.

The best way to remember to keep our promises is either to do them straightaway if we can, or, if not, to write them down so that we do not forget. The butler ought to have done that!

Are there things we have forgotten to do for God?

Our Bible dictionary

The Lord's Supper

At the Lord's Supper Christians eat bread and drink wine, as the first disciples did on the night the Lord Jesus was betrayed. The bread and the wine are symbols or pictures of the Lord Jesus' body and blood. Another name for the Lord's Supper is the Communion Service— 'communion' means fellowship or sharing. At the Lord's Supper Christians remember with gratitude how they share in the wonderful benefits that come to them through the Lord Jesus' death for them—especially the forgiveness of sins. They also look forward to the time when the Lord Jesus comes again to take all his people to be with him for ever.

Or for others? Is there a promise we have made which we need to keep? If so, let's do them today. Do not be like Mr Forgetful!

Where to read: Genesis 40

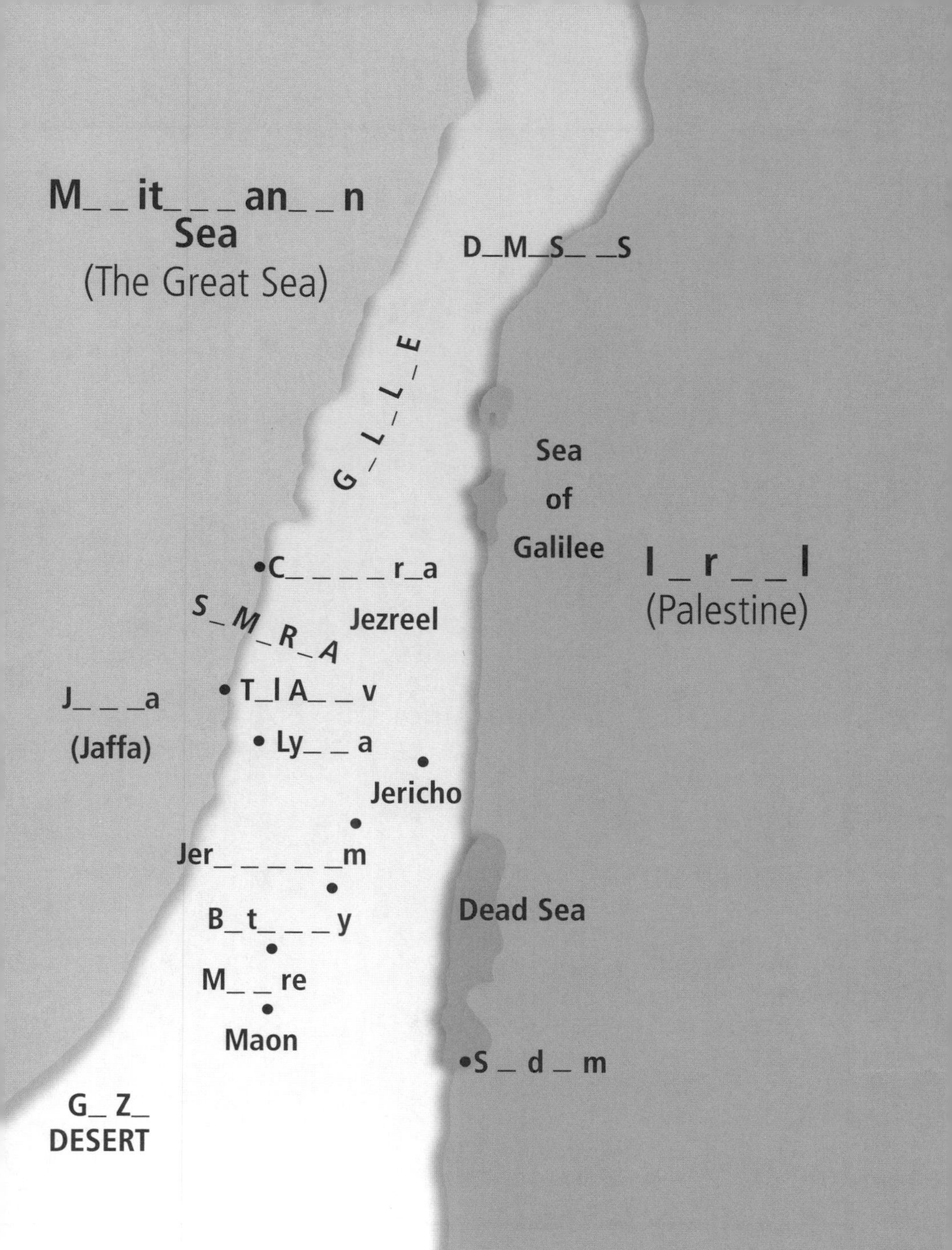

M_ _ it_ _ _ an_ _ n
Sea
(The Great Sea)

D_M_S_ _S

G_L_ _E

**Sea
of
Galilee**

I _ r _ _ l
(Palestine)

•C_ _ _ _ r_a

S_ M_ R_ A

Jezreel

J_ _ _a
(Jaffa)

• T_l A_ _ v

• Ly_ _ a

Jericho

Jer_ _ _ _ _m

B_ t_ _ _ y

Dead Sea

M_ _ re

Maon

•S _ d _ m

G_ Z_
DESERT

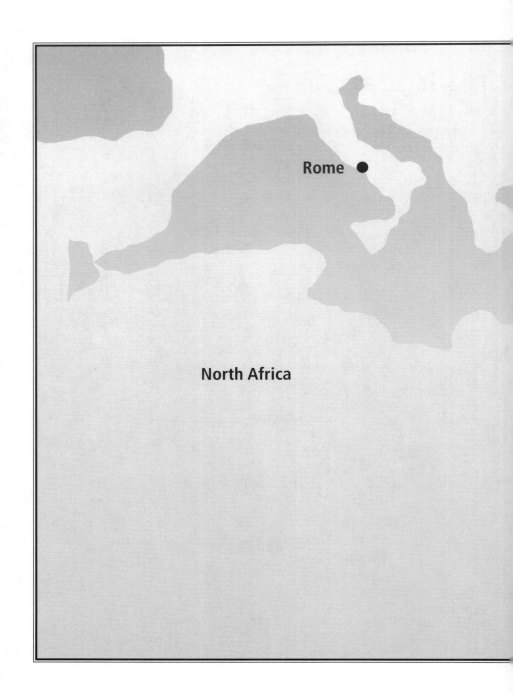

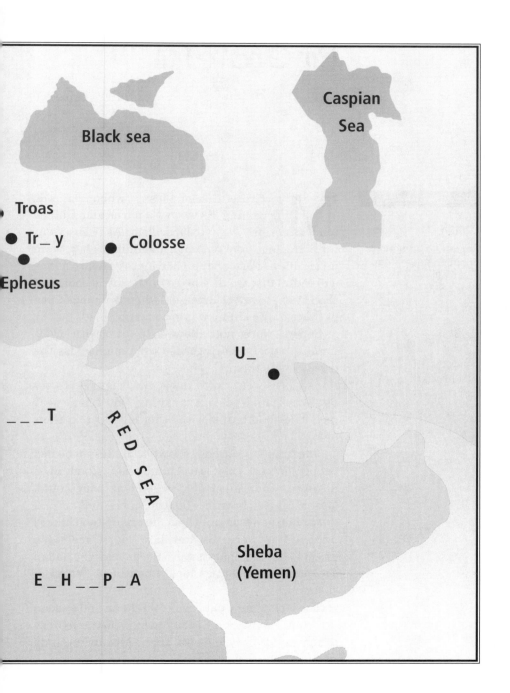

Caspian Sea

Black sea

Troas

Tr_ y

Colosse

Ephesus

U_

_ _ _ T

R E D   S E A

Sheba
(Yemen)

E _ H _ _ P _ A

Mr Grateful

Something to do

Mark the map!

See where Samaria is again on page 39 and find Galilee and write in its name.

Mr Grateful met Jesus when he was travelling between Samaria and Galilee on his way to Jerusalem. As Jesus went into a village ten sad men met him. They were miserable because they all had leprosy. Leprosy was a dreadful disease. It started with a little spot, and then it ate away at a person's hands or legs until perhaps only a stump was left.

Lepers were not allowed to live with their families and friends because they might pass the disease on to them.

As lepers went down the street, they had to cry out, 'Unclean! Unclean!' meaning 'Don't come near me!' They had to live with other lepers or on their own.

The ten lepers had heard that Jesus healed people. When they saw him, they stood at a distance, and called out as loud as they could, 'Jesus, Master, have pity on us!' And he did!

As soon as Jesus saw them, he understood how ill and sad they were. 'Go and show yourselves to the priests,' he said. Priests were the people who had to decide whether or not lepers had been healed of their leprosy.

The lepers did what Jesus told them, and as soon as they went on their way, their leprosy disappeared. They looked at their skin, and nothing

Can you draw?

Draw the nine lepers going home in the distance, and the one returning to say 'Thank you' to Jesus.

was wrong with it any longer! How excited they were! Perhaps they pinched themselves to make sure they were not dreaming!

One of them was not a Jew like the others, but a man from Samaria. When he saw that he was healed, he came back to Jesus, praising God in a loud voice. He fell flat on the ground in front of Jesus and thanked Him.

The Lord Jesus asked, 'Didn't I heal ten men? Where are the other nine? Was no one found to return and give praise to God except this foreigner?' Then Jesus said to the Samaritan, 'Stand up and go home; your faith has made you well.'

Ten lepers were made better but only one came back and said 'Thank you' and that was Mr Grateful.

Gratitude is remembering to say 'Thank you'. Do you write 'Thank you' letters? There are times when most of us do that, and especially, of course, at our birthdays and at Christmas when there are presents for which to be grateful.

Some people are quick to say 'Thank you'. A lady arrived by train at a London station. The first thing she did when she got off the train was to go to the train driver and say 'Thank you' to him for a safe and comfortable journey. He was very surprised, but pleased!

To whom do we say 'Thank you' most? Yes, to our parents and our friends, and to all who help us or do things for us.

Most of all, it is right to say 'Thank you' to God for sending the Lord Jesus to be our Saviour. We can never thank the Lord Jesus enough for dying for us.

Mr Grateful, the healed leper, came back and said 'Thank you'. One of the reasons we go to church every Sunday is to tell God in our hymns, songs and prayers, how grateful we are to him.

We show we are grateful to people by doing things for them in return, and by serving them. We show our gratitude to God too by serving him.

Nine lepers went home without saying 'Thank you', but one was grateful and he went back to Jesus and said so.

Are we like the nine or are we like Mr Grateful? Are we ungrateful or grateful people? Is there someone to whom we should say 'Thank you' today? Do we need to say 'Thank you' to God for something special?

Most important of all, have we ever said 'Thank you' to God for his gift of the Lord Jesus to be our Saviour?

Psalm 103, verse 2, tells us, 'Praise the Lord, O my soul, and forget not all his benefits.'

Where to read: Luke 17:11–19

Mr Humble

Mr Humble is the name we may give to a man the Lord Jesus spoke about in one of his stories. I wonder how you would describe a humble person? It is quite difficult, and perhaps it is easier to think of opposites.

The opposite of humble is proud. Proud people have big opinions of themselves, and humble people do not.

Perhaps you are good at Language or Maths, or at playing football or netball. If you are good at any of these things, you may be either proud or humble about it.

Proud people talk a lot about themselves. Humble people keep quiet about themselves. Proud people want others to know how much better or cleverer they are. They like comparing themselves with others.

Humble people do the opposite. They do not draw attention to themselves, and they do not enjoy comparing themselves with other people.

Let us listen to Jesus' story, and see if you can tell which of the two men Jesus talked about was Mr Humble.

Two men went up to the Temple in Jerusalem to pray: one was a very religious person, called a Pharisee, and the other was someone not liked very much because he was a tax-collector.

The Temple

The Temple was the special place in Jerusalem where the Jews worshipped God. The first Temple was built by King Solomon, and he followed the instructions God had given to his father, David. It was destroyed twice by invading armies and then rebuilt again. At the time of the Lord Jesus' ministry it was being rebuilt. The Temple was one of the wonders of the world. It was made of white marble, and was covered with a thin layer of gold. In AD 70 the Temple was destroyed again—this time by the Romans—and it has not been rebuilt.

The Pharisee stood up and prayed about himself: 'God,' he said, 'I thank you that I am not like all other men—robbers, evil-doers, adulterers—or even like this tax-collector. I go without food twice a week and give you a tenth of everything I earn.'

But the tax-collector stood at a distance. He would not even look up to heaven, but beat upon his chest with sorrow, and prayed, 'God be merciful to me, a sinner.'

Who was Mr Proud? And who was Mr Humble? The Pharisee was Mr Proud, and the tax-collector was Mr Humble.

The Lord Jesus said that Mr Proud went home unforgiven. He had not really been praying at all. Instead of praying, he had been talking to himself and any around him who may have been listening. But Mr Humble went home with all his sins completely forgiven by God.

The Bible tells us something about God which we always need to remember: 'God opposes the proud but gives grace to the humble.'

After telling his story, the Lord Jesus said, 'Everyone who thinks too much of himself will become a nobody, and whoever humbles himself will become a somebody.'

All the time we are proud, we cannot receive God's forgiveness for our sins. That was why the Pharisee went home unforgiven. If we are proud, God is not pleased with us, just as he was not pleased with the Pharisee.

The Pharisee thought God was pleased with him because he went often to church, prayed many prayers, and gave some of his money to God. But much more important to God was whether or not

the Pharisee was humble before him and others. The Lord Jesus, God's Son, who told this story, is the most wonderful Person who has ever lived in this world. Although so important he was never proud. He treated everyone with respect, and he kept on surprising his disciples by how humble he was, especially as one day he washed their feet, and later even went to the Cross to die in their place.

If you met Mr Proud and Mr Humble, which of them would you choose to be your friend? I think you would pick Mr Humble, because proud people are never attractive.

The Lord Jesus wants all his followers to remember his example and to walk in his footsteps. That is an important secret of being humble.

Where to read: Luke 18:9–14

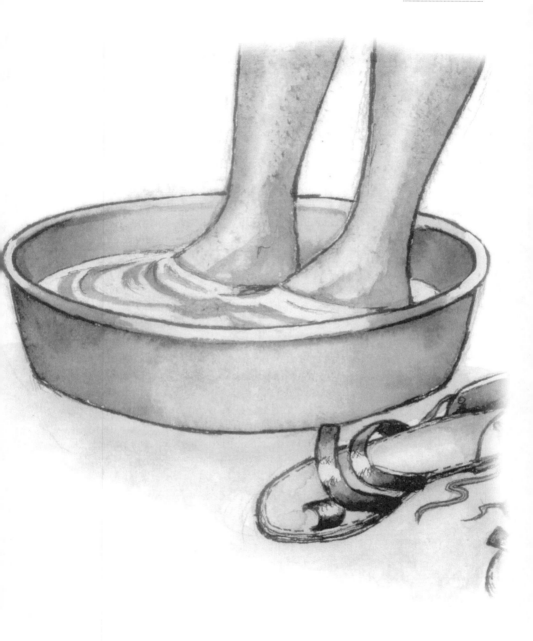

Miss Industrious

I hope you like learning new words. I wonder if you know what the word 'industrious' means? If anyone says you are industrious, it means that you work well and always do your best. It is a way of praising or congratulating you.

I expect your school has open evenings when your parents can go and talk to your teachers about you. Some schools give children reports to take home at the end of term or the school year. If your teachers say you are industrious, your parents will be pleased because it means you work hard. We cannot all be near the top of the class, but we can all do our best.

Miss Industrious lived in a small harbour town called Joppa on the coast of Israel. Its modern name is Jaffa, and it is just south of the city of Tel Aviv, which you will easily find on a map of Israel.

Her real name was Dorcas, a Greek word meaning 'a gazelle'. A 'gazelle' is a wild animal found in parts of Africa and Asia, and it looks like a deer.

The Bible tells us two important things about Dorcas: she was a follower of the Lord Jesus, and she was always helping others.

Dorcas heard the good news about the Lord Jesus' death for us, and how he rose again to be the Saviour and Lord of all who trust in him. She

Something to do

Mark the map!

Find Joppa and Tel Aviv on the map on page 39 and write in their names.

Our Bible dictionary

A disciple

A disciple is someone who wants to be taught by a teacher, and so it was a good name for the first followers of the Lord Jesus, and for all today who follow him. His disciples are those who trust him as their Saviour and live as he tells them to do. A disciple is another name for a Christian.

trusted in him as her Saviour, and she wanted to live to please him. True disciples like Dorcas listen to what the Lord Jesus says, and obey him. The Lord Jesus taught that if we love him, we will love one another. The way we behave and care for others shows whether or not we belong to him. The way Dorcas lived showed that she belonged to the Lord Jesus.

I do not know if she had much money, but she was always doing good and helping the poor. We do not have to be rich to help others, because there are things we may do to help people with our time and energy.

One of the things Dorcas loved doing was making clothes for those who could not afford to buy them. If she heard of a widow, or a boy or girl who did not have a father, she got out her needle and thread, and made shirts and coats to fit them exactly. As soon as

she finished one thing for one person, she would find something else to do for another.

Everyone who knew Dorcas loved her. She was so kind and thoughtful.

You can imagine how sad everyone was when one day they heard that Dorcas was ill. The sadness became all the greater when Dorcas died. Everyone who knew her was upset, and many cried. Some of her friends washed her body and prepared it for the funeral, and placed it in a room upstairs in her house.

But then someone said, 'Isn't Peter staying in Lydda?' Lydda was not far from Joppa. 'And didn't Peter heal Aeneas there, who had been bedridden for eight years? Let's send a message to Peter and get him to come to Joppa to see if he can help us.'

So they sent two men to Peter, with the message, 'Please hurry and come to us.'

Peter went with them at once, and when he arrived in Joppa he was taken to the upstairs room where Dorcas was. All the widows whom Dorcas had helped stood around him, and they pointed to the clothes they were wearing which Dorcas had made. They told him how industrious she had been for them, and in all her service for the Lord Jesus.

Peter asked them all to leave the room. He knelt down and prayed to God in the name of the Lord Jesus. Then he turned to Dorcas, and said, 'Dorcas, get up!' She opened her eyes, and when she saw Peter she sat up. Peter took her by the hand and helped her to her feet.

He called in all the Christians and the widows who had been so upset, and showed them she was now alive again. Their sadness was turned to happiness! They thanked God because they knew it

Something to do

Mark the map!
Find Lydda on the map on page 39 and write in its name.

Can you draw?

Draw the widows and children showing Peter the things Dorcas had made for them.

Our Bible dictionary

A Christian

People who believe in the Lord Jesus were first called Christians as a nick-name. Christians are those who belong to the Lord Jesus because they know that he died for their sins and rose again to be their Saviour and Lord. It is another name for those who follow the Lord Jesus.

was not Peter's own power that had restored Dorcas to life, but the power of the Lord Jesus, in whose name Peter had prayed.

The news about Dorcas spread all over Joppa, and many people believed in the Lord Jesus. And Dorcas went on being industrious for the Lord Jesus as she continued to do good and help the poor.

What about us? Are we industrious or lazy? It is easy to be lazy at school, and not to work hard. It is also easy not to be bothered about helping other people, especially the lonely and those who are ill. When we believe in the Lord Jesus, and receive him as our Saviour, something happens deep inside us. The Lord Jesus comes to live within us by his Spirit, and he teaches and helps us to be kind and

thoughtful to others, and to work hard at it—to be industrious.

The Bible says, 'Whatever you do, work at it with all your heart, as working for the Lord, not for men'. We cannot all be clever, and we cannot all be rich, but we can all work hard at helping others.

In lots of churches in the world Dorcas clubs or societies have been formed, named after Miss Industrious. The members commit themselves to doing kind and useful things to help others. Without joining a Dorcas club or society, with God's help we can all be like her.

Where to read: Acts 9:32-43; Colossians 3:23

Mr Jealous

Are you ever jealous? It is not something we like to admit, but it may often show in our actions. Are jealous people attractive? No, they are not! The Mr Jealous I want us to think about was a king. Now we would not think that a king would need to be jealous of anyone, but this king was. Mr Jealous's real name was Saul, and he was the first king of Israel. He was very tall and strong. But I am sorry to say that he became jealous of someone much younger than himself, a young man called David.

Saul had not always been jealous of David. When he first met him, he liked him and soon grew to love him. He first admired David when he volunteered to fight against Goliath when everyone else was afraid to do so. He saw David run out to meet Goliath, and watched as he hurled one small stone from his shepherd's sling at Goliath's head with deadly accuracy.

Saul ought to have liked David all the more when he became the best friend of Jonathan, Saul's son.

Whatever Saul gave David to do, he did well. It was not long before Saul made him commander of all his troops.

But David's great success in battles soon made Saul jealous. When Saul and David came home from war, the women came out from all the towns of

Israel to cheer. They sang and danced for joy, and played their tambourines and other musical instruments. As they danced, they sang: 'Saul has killed his thousands, and David his tens of thousands.'

Saul was angry when he heard this. 'For David they claim tens of thousands,' he thought, 'but me with only thousands. The next thing they will be wanting is for David to be their king.'

The Bible says that 'from that time on Saul kept a jealous eye on David'. Jealousy made him do lots of silly and stupid things. First, it made him angry, and when we let ourselves get angry, we may do things we are sorry about afterwards.

One day David was playing his harp for Saul, as he often did. Suddenly Saul threw his spear at David, but missed. This happened at least two other times.

In the end Saul decided he would try to get rid of David. First, he thought he would give David a dangerous battle to fight against his country's enemies, the Philistines, so that they might kill him. But his plan failed.

Saul then told his son Jonathan and all his servants to kill David, but Jonathan warned David so that he escaped.

Sometimes Saul realised that his jealousy was wrong, and he then promised not to hurt David any more. But soon his jealousy became so strong again that he broke his promises.

God did not let Saul capture David. God is never pleased when we are jealous.

I wonder if we are sometimes jealous? It can happen on other people's birthdays. When they open their presents, we may be jealous of the gifts they receive. Or perhaps our friends play the piano or football better than we do, and instead of being glad we find fault with them, because deep down we are jealous.

Someone may have a friend whom we would like to have as our friend, and we may be nasty to that person because we are jealous.

Jealousy took control of Saul's life because he did not listen to God. Once upon a time God had been with Saul in all that he did, and helped him, just as he helped David. But in the end God left Saul all alone and stopped helping him, and his jealousy then just got worse and worse. The Bible says that jealousy is even more horrible than anger.

How can we stop being jealous? To begin with, there are things we need to know about jealousy. Jealousy is something Satan, the devil, loves to see in us because it makes us like him.

Do you remember?

Satan

Satan is another name for the devil.

He is against all that is good, and he is behind everything that is evil in the world. He brought men and women under his power by tempting Adam and Eve to disobey God so that they and we deserve to die and to be separated from God.

The Bible does not explain why God allowed Satan to have such power, but it tells us the good news that the Lord Jesus came into the world as a human being so that he could break Satan's power: the Lord Jesus did this when he died on the Cross as the Substitute for sinners, and then rose again.

When the Lord Jesus returns, all Satan's power will be taken away from him for ever.

Prayer

Prayer is talking to God, and is part of the special relationship we have with God when we trust in the Lord Jesus as our Saviour and come to God in his Name. Prayer is asking God for the things that we know he wants for others and ourselves. In what we call the Lord's Prayer, the Lord Jesus teaches us the kind of things we should ask God for when we pray. See Matthew 6:9–13. God wants us to talk to him about everything that worries or concerns us.

Jealousy is sin, and is one of the things for which the Lord Jesus Christ had to accept the punishment we deserve when he died on the Cross so that we could be forgiven.

When we become Christians, jealousy belongs to the way we used to behave before we were Christians, and not to the way we now want to live as the Lord Jesus' disciples.

There are two things we can do to help us overcome jealousy. First, we can pray for the people of whom we are jealous, asking God to help us to love them and to care about them. Then instead of being jealous of their birthday presents, we will be glad that they are pleased with the gifts they

True or False?

Place a 'T' where and a 'F' where false against these sentences:

If we are jealous we will be cross when others do better than we do.

If we are jealous we will be quick to congratulate others when they succeed.

If we are jealous people will want us as their friend.

receive. Rather than criticising them, we will praise and encourage them.

The second thing we can do is to ask God to help us to be happy with what we have. We do not need to be jealous of other people. God made us as we are with our own gifts and abilities. When we add up all the good things he gives us each day, we realise how stupid we are to envy what other people have.

Where to read: 1 Samuel 18:1–17; Proverbs 27:4

Mr Kindness

Something to do

Mark the map!

Find where Samaria, Jerusalem and Jericho are on the map on page 77 and write in their names.

Do you remember?

The Temple

Please turn to page 47 if you have forgotten!

I wonder how you would describe a kind person? Can you think of someone who is kind? He or she will be thoughtful, generous and always willing to help you.

Kind people put others before themselves. I cannot tell you the name of the Mr Kindness we are going to think about, although I know he came from Samaria. The Lord Jesus told a story about his kindness.

A man was going down from Jerusalem to Jericho, when he fell into the hands of robbers. They stripped him of his clothes, beat him and went away, leaving the poor man half-dead, lying in the road.

It so happened that a priest was going down the same road, and when he saw the man, he passed by on the other side.

So too, a man who helped in the Temple in Jerusalem, called a Levite, came to the place, saw the wounded man, but passed by on the other side, just like the priest.

But a Samaritan, as he travelled along the same road, came to where the man was. When he saw him, he felt very sorry for him. He went up to him, and cleaned and bandaged his cuts and bruises.

Then he put the man on his own donkey, brought him to a place where travellers might spend the

Can you draw?

Draw the Samaritan helping the man who fell into the hands of robbers. You might draw the priest and the Levite in the distance, walking away.

night, and cared for him. The next day he took out two silver coins and gave them to the owner of the place. 'Look after him, please,' he said, 'and when I return, I will pay the bill for any extra expense you may have had.'

Which of those three men deserves to be called Mr Kindness? Yes, the Samaritan. He was thoughtful, helpful, and generous. He put the poor injured man's needs before his own business.

The kindest person who has ever lived in this world is our Lord Jesus. He went about doing kind things. He was so kind that he even died on the Cross for us, to make it possible for our sins to be forgiven. When we trust him as our Saviour we want to be like him, and that helps to make us kind.

There is a story about two brothers, one of whom had a family and the other had none. They both

sowed a field of wheat. On the evening after the beginning of the harvest, the older brother said to his wife, 'My younger brother is unable to bear the heat and work of the day as I am; I will get up, take some of my sheaves and place them with his without his knowing.'

The younger brother had the same kind thought. He said to himself, 'My older brother has a family, and I have none. I will get up, take some of my sheaves and put them with his.'

Imagine how surprised they were the next day when they saw that their stacks of sheaves were more or less exactly the same, in spite of what they had done!

This happened for several nights. Then each decided to keep guard and solve the mystery. They did so, and to their surprise met each other half-way between their piles of sheaves with their arms full! They were being kind to one another, and they had not wanted to show off about it.

A boy from a poor family went into a butcher's for his mother. As he was leaving, the man who owned the shop said, 'Have you got a dog at home?' He gave the boy a big bag as large as the boy's head.

When his mother opened the scraps, she said, 'You've picked up somebody else's parcel.'

'No,' he said, 'I didn't. He put it right into my hands.'

'But it is all little chunks of good red meat,' his mother said. 'He did not intend it for the dog at all. Everybody is so kind to us!'

Kindness is love and thoughtfulness in action. Can you think of ways in which you can be kind?

Perhaps new children join your class at school. It is kind to show them round, and include them in your games. Teachers usually know the thoughtful children whom they may best ask to look after someone new.

To show kindness to others is something which always pleases the Lord Jesus.

Where to read: Luke 10:25–37

Mrs Laughter

Can you laugh? I am sure you can! There are different kinds of laughter. We laugh at funny stories and jokes. We laugh when something happy or exciting happens, or when we play games with our friends.

Some laughter can be unkind. People may laugh at someone who is in difficulty, or who perhaps looks ugly or is strangely dressed. Laughter like that is cruel.

Sometimes we laugh, and cannot stop laughing! A girl, called Molly, went to school in Glasgow. One day the teacher went out of the class during an art lesson, and she left the children to draw an orange with their crayons.

The girl next to Molly had a tiny tube filled with 'hundreds and thousands', those little coloured sugar dots, no bigger than a pinhead, that are used for putting on the top of cakes. They had stuck together, and refused to come out of the tube, however hard she sucked.

Trying to help her, Molly hit the bottom of the tube sharply, and the whole lot shot out in a wet blob, and landed right in the middle of her drawing.

As they watched, the coloured sugar began to run, and in a minute the orange looked as if it had a horrible disease!

They dared not touch it in case they got it all over

their clothes, and they knew the teacher would be furious with them for spoiling the page in their drawing book.

They looked at one another and burst into peals of laughter which they simply could not control. The girls in the back row crowded round to see what they were laughing at.

They held their sides, and explained what had happened between bursts of giggles. It was infectious and soon the whole class was laughing.

Suddenly the door opened, and the teacher walked in. 'What is the meaning of this?' she demanded. The rest of the class fell silent but Molly and her neighbour could not stop laughing. Tears of laughter fell down their cheeks. They shook, and their voices squeaked as they tried to speak. That was the first time Molly really got into trouble at school!

Let me tell you about Mrs Laughter, whose laughter was very different and secret—or so she thought!

Have you ever had unexpected visitors at home? Abraham and Sarah did. The Lord himself appeared to Abraham near Mamre while Abraham was sitting at the entrance to his tent during the hottest part of the day.

Abraham looked up, and saw three men standing close by. It was the Lord and two companions. When Abraham saw them, he sprang up, and ran to welcome them.

Abraham said, 'Sirs, please don't pass my home by without stopping. I'll be pleased to get you some water, so you may wash your feet and rest under this tree.'

Then he added, 'Let me get you something to eat, so you can be refreshed and then go on your way.'

'Very well,' they answered, 'do as you say.'

So Abraham hurried into the tent to Sarah.

'Quick,' he said, 'we've got visitors. Please bake some fresh bread for them.'

Something to do

Mark the map!

Find where Mamre is on the map on page 77 and write in its name.

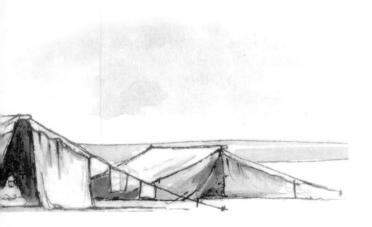

Chapter 12

Can you draw?

A picture of Abraham looking after his guests and talking with them, with Sarah listening at the door of the tent.

Then he ran to his herd and picked out a calf that was tender and fat, and gave it to a servant, who hurried to get it ready. After a little while he brought some cream and milk, and the meat that had been cooked, and set them before his guests. While they ate, Abraham stood near them under a tree, ready to get anything they needed.

Now Sarah, Abraham's wife, had no children. It made her very sad. Ever since she had married Abraham she had looked forward to having a family of her own, especially as God had promised to make Abraham's family grow until it would be too large to count. But the years passed and still Sarah had not had a baby.

When Abraham was a hundred years old, and Sarah ninety, God promised Abraham, 'I will bless Sarah and will give you a son by her.'

Abraham laughed with joy and astonishment, and God repeated his promise, 'Sarah will bear you a son by this time next year.'

It was soon afterwards that this visit of the Lord to Abraham took place. Abraham had told Sarah what God had promised, but Sarah had not believed it possible because they were so old.

While Abraham's guests were eating their meal, they said to Abraham, 'Where is your wife, Sarah?'

'She is there in the tent,' he replied.

Then the Lord said to Abraham, 'Next year I will give Sarah and you a son.'

Now Sarah was listening at the door to the tent. Do you know what she did? She laughed! She laughed to herself, and said, 'That's impossible! I'm too old to have a baby!'

Sarah was not only Mrs Laughter, she was also Mrs Listener!

Her laugh was a laugh of unbelief. She did not believe what God said.

But it was also a laugh to herself. She thought no one knew about her secret laugh.

The Lord said to Abraham, 'Why did Sarah laugh and say, "Will I really have a child now that I am old?" Is anything too hard for the Lord? Just as I told you Sarah will have a son next year.'

Sarah was afraid and she lied and said, 'I did not laugh.'

But the Lord, who knows everything, said, 'Yes, you did laugh.'

What do you think happened the following year? At the time God promised, Sarah had a baby son, and she then laughed with joy. I wonder if you can

How old was Abraham and how old was Sarah when Isaac was born?

guess what Sarah said? 'God has brought me laughter,' she said, 'and everyone who hears about this will laugh with me.' Then she added, 'Who would have dreamed that I would ever have a baby at my age, and give Abraham a baby in his old age?'

But here is another question. What do you think Sarah called her son? She called him Isaac which means 'Laughter'!

Every time Sarah used his name, she remembered God's kindness to her, and how he had made her laugh with joy even though she had laughed because she had not thought God's promise possible.

Sarah discovered that God can do the impossible! Nothing is too hard for him.

When God tells us wonderful things in his Book, the Bible, do we laugh secretly, not believing them to be possible? Or do we believe what God says?

The most wonderful promise God makes is that he will forgive us our sins and prepare a home in heaven for us if we trust in his Son, the Lord Jesus, who died for sinners on the Cross.

Do you believe that promise? If you believe it, God will fill your life with joy, and with laughter of the right kind!

Where to read: Genesis 18:1–15; Genesis 21:1–8

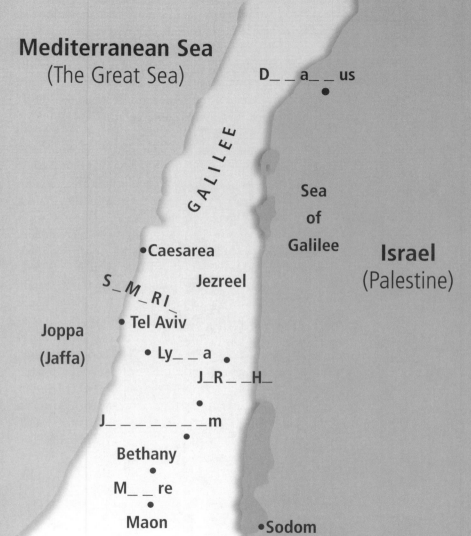

Mediterranean Sea
(The Great Sea)

D_ _ a_ _ us

GALILEE

Sea
of
Galilee

•Caesarea

Israel
(Palestine)

Jezreel

S_ M_ RI

• Tel Aviv

Joppa
(Jaffa)

• Ly_ _ a

J_R_ _H_

J_ _ _ _ _ _ _m

Bethany

M_ _ re

Maon

•Sodom

GAZA
DESERT

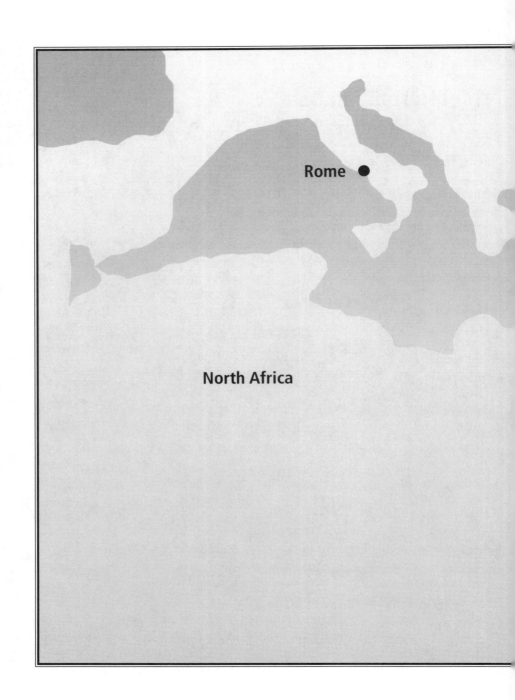

Rome ●

North Africa

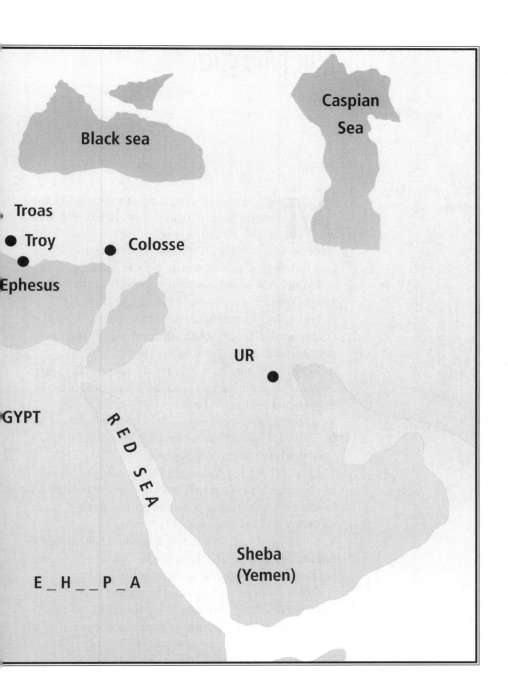

Black sea

Caspian Sea

Troas

Troy

Colosse

Ephesus

UR

GYPT

RED SEA

Sheba (Yemen)

E _ H _ _ P _ A

Mr Magic

Magic is the power to do clever tricks that people cannot usually do. In many parts of the world, especially in some of the forests where Indian tribes live, witch-doctors practise magic; and so too do people called witches.

Magic is a word we also use to describe what magicians do.

Have you been to a birthday party where a conjuror did tricks that amazed you? You have probably wondered how he did them!

Conjurors' magic is not really magic. They are clever with their hands, and they know how to make us think something is happening when it is not!

Unfortunately, some people believe in magic, and in spells. They often wear charms around their necks or have them as bracelets.

Lots of people read their horoscopes in the newspaper. They think that what is going to happen to them in the future depends on the date of their birthday and the position of the stars.

Some men and women will never walk under a ladder, or allow you to cross the knives when you are getting out the cutlery to lay a table.

Others will go to a fair and pay a fortune teller to tell them their fortunes, or the palmist to read their hands and tell them what is going to happen in the future.

Do you remember?

Satan

Satan is another name for the devil.

He is against all that is good, and he is behind everything that is evil in the world. He brought men and women under his power by tempting Adam and Eve to disobey God so that they and we deserve to die and to be separated from God.

The Bible does not explain why God allowed Satan to have such power, but it tells us the good news that the Lord Jesus came into the world as a human being so that he could break Satan's power: the Lord Jesus did this when he died on the Cross as the Substitute for sinners, and then rose again.

When the Lord Jesus returns, all Satan's power will be taken away from him for ever.

Bookshops sell books about magic, and some people, including children, foolishly play with ouija boards.

In a ouija board the letters of the alphabet are arranged in a semi-circle with the words 'yes' or 'no' at either end. Then a glass is turned upside down and people place a finger on the glass asking a spirit to move the glass. They treat ouija as a game, but really it is dangerous and wrong.

There is nothing wrong with conjurors' magic if they only want to entertain us, and make us guess how they do the clever things they do. Many of us like doing tricks and puzzles. But magic is wrong when people believe in it, and allow it to tell them what to do.

Satan, our great enemy, is behind all the magic people believe in. He does not want people to trust in God but to trust in him instead.

Magic goes back a long time. Right at the

beginning of the Bible, God told his people that they were not to imitate the horrible things they saw other nations do. No one was to do magic by the power of evil spirits. They were not to cast spells, or to try to be in touch with people who were dead. Anyone who does such things displeases God.

Sometimes people talk about 'Black Magic', and that is magic where men and women deliberately call upon the devil either to worship him or to ask him to do things for them.

The real name of Mr Magic in the Bible was Simon. He lived in Samaria in the first century.

Christians had arrived in Samaria when they had had to leave Jerusalem when they were persecuted. They immediately told the good news of Jesus to the people there. One of those Christians was Philip.

The people of Samaria had never heard the good news about Jesus before. Not only did Philip preach about Jesus, but God gave him power to perform miracles in the name of Jesus.

The Samaritans listened carefully to what Philip said, and saw the miracles he did. Evil spirits made a loud noise as they came out of many demon-possessed people. Those who were paralysed or crippled were healed. There was great joy in the city.

Simon had practised magic for a long time in Samaria. He was really famous for his magic and he cast all kinds of spells.

He boasted that he was someone great, and everyone admired him, and said, 'This man has great power!'

But when people believed the good news Philip brought about the Lord Jesus, they stopped taking

Something to do

Mark the map!

Find where Samaria, the Gaza Desert and Ethiopia are on the maps on pages 122 and 123 and write in their names.

Do you remember?

Persecute, Persecution

To persecute is to treat people cruelly and unfairly usually because of what they believe. From the beginning Christians have often been persecuted because of their faith. See what the Lord Jesus says in John 15:20–21. Persecution of Christians still happens in many parts of the world.

Apostles

An apostle is someone sent out as a messenger. Although it can mean any sort of messenger, it describes the men the Lord Jesus first chose to be his special followers so that they might be eye-witnesses of his life and work, and especially of his resurrection.

any notice of Simon. Soon Simon said that he believed in Jesus.

Simon followed Philip everywhere, and was amazed at the great signs and miracles Philip could do, without any of the magic and tricks Simon always used.

Two of the apostles—Peter and John—came down to Samaria to see what God had been doing through Philip. Simon, Mr Magic, saw the great power that God had given them too through his Holy Spirit. He then did something foolish and silly. He offered Peter and John money if they would give him the power they had!

God's power cannot be bought with money. God gives his Holy Spirit to those who trust in the Lord Jesus, and who want to live to please him.

Peter told off Simon right away. 'May your money die with you,' he said, 'because you thought you could buy God's gift of his Spirit with money. Your heart is not right before God. Repent of this wickedness and pray for God's forgiveness. Perhaps he will forgive you for having such a thought in your heart. I can see there is jealousy and sin in your heart.'

'Please pray for me,' Simon asked, 'so that the bad things you have said may not happen to me'.

Christians do not have to do silly things like 'touching wood', or keeping their fingers crossed, or avoiding walking under ladders. We do not have to be afraid of magic or of Satan because the Lord Jesus has overcome all the powers of evil for us. When he rose again from the dead, he was victorious over Satan and all evil powers.

The lesson of Mr Magic, Simon, is that we should not have anything to do with magic, but trust in the Lord Jesus and in him alone. When we trust in him, we do not need to be afraid of anything or anyone!

Where to read: Acts 8:4–24; Deuteronomy 18:9–13

Mr Nobody

If we call someone a 'nobody' we are saying that he or she is not very important. A 'somebody' is a person whom everyone takes notice of, like a king or queen, or a prime minister or president, or an international footballer or tennis player.

When Mr and Miss Somebody arrive at an airport or railway station, important people go out to meet them, and a red carpet is put down.

But when Mr Nobody arrives, no one takes any notice, and no preparations are made to welcome him. A wonderful truth the Bible teaches is that no one is a 'nobody' to God. Everyone is important to him! When the Lord Jesus was here on earth, He showed that little children or beggars in the street are as important to God as kings and queens, prime ministers, presidents and politicians.

Perhaps you feel sometimes that you are a nobody? As you come in the front door of your home, maybe your father asks your mother, 'Who is that?' 'Oh, nobody,' she answers. And she then tells him that it is only you!

Let me tell you about Mr Nobody. That name was given to him at least twice. The first time was when an important visitor came to his home while he was out in the fields looking after his father's sheep.

At that time King Saul was king over Israel. He had failed to please God as a king, and God was going to choose another ruler for the people. God's servant—a man called Samuel—was sent by God to

the home of Jesse because one of Jesse's sons was to be the next king.

Samuel asked Jesse to bring all his sons to meet him. Jesse did so with just one son missing. Can you guess who it was he did not call to come to meet Samuel? Yes, someone whom he thought was Mr Nobody, his youngest son, David.

Since David was his youngest son, who spent his time looking after his father's sheep, Jesse did not think it important for Samuel to meet him.

One by one Jesse's sons were introduced to Samuel, until all seven of the eight had been brought to him. Samuel was puzzled, because he knew that the Lord had not chosen any one of them.

So Samuel asked Jesse, 'Are these all the sons you have?'

'There is the youngest,' replied Jesse, 'but he is looking after the sheep.'

Samuel said, 'Send for him straightaway. We will not sit down and eat until he arrives.'

So Jesse sent for David, and introduced him to Samuel. He looked a healthy and strong young man. Then the Lord said to Samuel, 'This is the one!'

The youngest son whom everyone thought was a nobody God made into a somebody!

Not long afterwards the same thing happened again! David continued to look after his sheep because it was still a secret that he was to be the next king.

A war was going on between Israel and the Philistines, and three of David's brothers joined Saul's army to fight against them.

The Philistines had a great champion fighter called Goliath. He was over nine feet tall, and everyone looked small besides him.

He had a strong helmet on his head, and wore a suit of armour. On his legs he wore bronze leggings, and a javelin was slung on his back.

He carried a huge spear, and its iron point was large and strong. Ahead of him went his shield-bearer. All the men of Israel's army were afraid of him. Goliath stood and shouted at them, 'Why do our whole armies fight? Am I not a Philistine, and are you not servants of Saul? Choose a man and have him come and fight me. If he is able to kill me, we will become your subjects. But if I overcome him and kill him, you will become our subjects and serve us.' Then he said, 'Today I challenge all the soldiers of Israel! Give me a man, and let us fight each other.'

As soon as Saul's soldiers heard this they were terrified, including David's brothers.

At this time Jesse, David's father, sent David to visit his brothers to find out how they were and to take them some food.

Early in the morning, David left his sheep with another shepherd, loaded up all the food he was to take, and did as his father had told him.

He reached the army camp just as Goliath came out again and repeated his challenge. When the soldiers saw Goliath, they ran away.

David's brothers were cross and rude when they found him waiting for them at their tents. 'Why have you come here?' his oldest brother asked. 'You have just come down to watch the battle.'

That was not true because it was David's father who had told him to visit his brothers. But David took no notice. Instead he went to King Saul and said, 'Don't give in to Goliath. I'll go and fight him!'

You can guess, I expect, what was in Saul's mind. 'You are a nobody!' was what Saul thought. He said, 'You are only a boy, and Goliath has been a fighting man since he was a youth.'

David replied, 'Your servant has been looking after his father's sheep. When a lion and a bear came and carried off sheep from the flock, I went after them, struck them, and rescued the sheep from their mouth. When they turned on me, I seized them by their hair, and killed them. Your servant has killed both the lion and the bear. The same will happen to this Philistine because he has defied the armies of the living God.'

He then added, 'The Lord who delivered me from the paw of the lion and the paw of the bear will deliver me from the hand of this Philistine.'

Saul had no answer to what David said. All he could say was, 'Go, and the Lord be with you!'

At first Saul tried to put his own armour on David, but it was too large. Have you ever dressed up in your parents' clothes and found them much too big for you? So David went to fight against Goliath without any of Saul's armour.

He took his shepherd's staff in his hand, chose five

smooth stones from a stream, put them in his bag, and with his sling in his hand, went towards Goliath.

Can you guess what the champion Goliath thought as he saw David? He looked David up and down, and saw he was only a boy. He thought him a nobody!

But David put a stone in his sling, and with one stone he struck the Philistine in the centre of his forehead, and he fell down on the ground—dead!

David—Mr Nobody—became a champion, and later, David, Mr Nobody, became a king.

There is a verse in the Bible which tells us that God deliberately chooses the nobodies of this world to show people who think they are somebodies how foolish they are to be so proud.

When we trust in God, and do what he wants, we can do things the world thinks impossible!

People who do not trust and obey God achieve little that lasts, even if they are thought important 'somebodies'. But all who trust and obey God can do great things to please him and help others, even if the world thinks they are 'nobodies'!

No one is a Mr, Mrs, Master or Miss Nobody to God. The Lord Jesus, God's Son, taught that all of us are important to God, and he showed it by what he did. He left heaven, and came and lived in this world and died for ordinary people like us, who need a Saviour.

When we trust in the Lord Jesus as our Saviour, God makes us into people who are very special to him. He makes those whom the world may think 'nobodies' into 'somebodies'—people who can live to please him.

Where to read: 1 Samuel 16:1–13; 1 Samuel 17:1–51; 1 Corinthians 1:27

Can you draw?

A picture of David fighting Goliath, with all the soldiers of both armies watching.

Mr Obedient

O bedience is something we all have to learn. What does it mean to be obedient? Yes, it means to do as we are told! I wonder if you have ever had a puppy? One of the first things we try to teach a puppy is obedience. It is important that it should learn to do as it is told, not just for our sake but for its own. If it does not learn to obey, it may not do as it is told in dangerous traffic, and then perhaps be hurt or even run over.

To whom then should we be obedient? First, we should obey God. God gives us instructions and directions in his Word. As we do what he tells us in the Bible, we are obedient to him.

To whom else should we be obedient? We should obey our parents and our teachers at school.

Let me tell you about Mr Obedient. His real name was Ananias. There are three men called Ananias in the Acts of the Apostles. This is not the Ananias who sadly tried to lie to God and it is not the Ananias who was high priest. The Ananias who was Mr Obedient lived in an important and busy city called Damascus.

He may not have lived there all his life because Christians moved to places like Damascus when they had to leave Jerusalem because of the persecution against Christians.

Many Christians were ill-treated for their faith

Something to do

Mark the map!

Find where Damascus is on page 122 and write in its name.

Do you remember?

Persecution

see Our Bible dictionary, page 30.

A Christian

People who believe in the Lord Jesus were first called Christians as a nick-name. Christians are those who belong to the Lord Jesus because they know that he died for their sins and rose again to be their Saviour and Lord.

It is another name for those who follow the Lord Jesus.

Our Bible dictionary

Conversion

To convert is to change, and conversion describes what happens when we become Christians: we turn from going our own way to going God's way. When we are converted, we turn from our sins, we believe in the Lord Jesus as our Saviour, and we want to spend the rest of our life pleasing the Lord Jesus who died and rose again for us.

after the death of Stephen, one of the early Christians. The person behind the dreadful things that happened was Saul, who came from the town of Tarsus in Turkey. He went from house to house and dragged off men and women who believed in Jesus and put them in prison.

Ananias may have been one of the Christians who escaped from Jerusalem. Or he may have become a Christian through those believers who came to his city and witnessed about Jesus.

But something wonderful happened to Saul! He was on his way to Damascus to do there the dreadful things he had done to Christians in Jerusalem. But suddenly the Lord Jesus met Saul, and showed him that he was alive. Saul saw then that he had been wrong in all his thoughts about Jesus, and he was converted.

Saul understood for the first time why the Lord Jesus had come into the world. He believed now that he had died and risen again so that he—and people like us—might be forgiven and know God as Father. Saul became a Christian.

When Saul tried to open his eyes after meeting the Lord Jesus, he found that he could not see anything. So he had to be led by the hand to Damascus. For three days he was blind, and he did not eat or drink anything.

This was when Ananias proved himself to be Mr Obedient.

The Lord Jesus spoke to Ananias in a vision. 'Ananias,' he called. Ananias replied, 'Yes, Lord.' That answer was important. Mr Obedient is someone who calls Jesus 'Lord', and means it. Christians not only believe the Lord

Do you remember?

Lord

Besides being the ordinary word to describe a person's boss or a slave's master, the word 'Lord' is a special name kept for God alone in the Bible. 'Lord' was the name or title the first followers of Jesus used when they spoke to him or about him. When we say 'Jesus is Lord' we are saying that he is God, and that he is worthy of our worship, service and obedience.

Jesus died for their sins, but they also know that he is God, the Lord, and the Person we ought always to obey. If we are Mr or Miss Obedient, we will call Jesus 'Lord' too, and really mean it!

The Lord Jesus told Ananias, 'Go to Judas' house on Straight Street, and ask for a man from Tarsus, named Saul, and you will find him praying. In a vision he has seen a man named Ananias come and place his hands on him to restore his sight.'

Now Ananias—Mr Obedient—thought this very difficult. 'Lord,' answered Ananias, 'I have heard many reports about this man and all the harm he has done to your people in Jerusalem. And he has power and permission from the chief priests to arrest all who call on your name.'

I can guess what Ananias was thinking. Saul had come to Damascus to arrest Christians and put them in prison, and here was the Lord Jesus telling Ananias to go to him!

The Lord said to Ananias, 'Go! I have chosen this man to take my message to the nations and their kings, and to the Jewish people. I will show him how much he must suffer for my name.'

But Mr Obedient wanted to obey, no matter how hard it might be. Ananias went because he was Mr Obedient.

Whatever God says to us, we should do! And if we love the Lord Jesus, we will! God always wants to speak to us as we read his Word, the Bible, or listen to it being taught or preached at church and Sunday School. It will instruct us about things like honesty, respect for our parents, working hard at school, and many other good things. We please God when we gladly obey what his Word says.

Ananias went to Judas' house in Straight Street, where he found Saul. He placed his hands on him, and said, 'Brother Saul, the Lord Jesus, who appeared to you on the road, has sent me so that you may see again, and be filled with the Holy Spirit.'

At once something like scales fell from Saul's eyes, and he could see again. He got up and showed his faith in the Lord Jesus by being baptised. Then he started eating again, and was strengthened.

Do you remember Ananias' first words to Saul? 'Brother Saul' was what he said. Ananias welcomed Saul into God's family, because he now trusted in the Lord Jesus. The people Saul had come to Damascus to persecute had become his brothers and sisters!

The name by which we best know Saul is Paul. He later became the famous apostle.

God has lots of good things and lovely surprises for those who obey him.

We do not read of Ananias anywhere else in the Bible. He comes into this story about Saul and then he disappears. But he had done what God asked, and that is what Mr Obedient always does.

The Lord Jesus said, 'If you love me, keep my commandments.' All who love the Lord Jesus want to be Mr, Mrs, Master or Miss Obedient!

Where to read: Acts 9:1–19; John 14:15

Verses to look up

Fill in the blanks –

If we love the Lord Jesus we will:
o – – – what he commands (John 14:15).
l – – – one another (John 13:34).
l – – – our e – – – – – – (Matthew 5:44).

Mrs Peacemaker

Do you quarrel? I hope not. But all of us have to admit that we have sometimes quarrelled with others. We may have said to a friend, 'I'm not going to speak to you again' or 'I'm not going to play with you any more.'

Have you ever tried to stop a fight or quarrel? When people quarrel they may refuse to speak to each other afterwards. They may even want to hurt or harm one another. Quarrels always make people unhappy.

The kind of person we need most when there are quarrels or arguments is a peacemaker. A peacemaker is someone who comes and helps us to try to make peace. That is what Mrs Peacemaker did.

Her real name was Abigail. The Bible tells us she was both intelligent and beautiful. She was

attractive not only in looks but also in character. But she had a husband who was quite the opposite. His name was Nabal, and he was sullen and grumpy, mean and stingy. He did not have many friends—perhaps even none—because he was so awkward and selfish.

Nabal was very wealthy and he possessed a thousand goats and three thousand sheep, and he employed many shepherds to look after them. Once his shepherds were looking for pasture for their flocks and they met David and his men. David was kind to them, and protected them from danger all the time they were with him.

One day David moved into the Desert of Maon, near where Nabal and Abigail lived. David and his men needed food to eat. He remembered how he had met Nabal's shepherds in the desert and had helped

Something to do

Mark the map!
Find where Maon is on the map on page 122 and write in its name.

them. So he sent ten young men and said to them, 'Go up to Nabal and greet him in my name. Say to him, "Long life to you! Good health to you and your household! And good health to all that is yours! Now I hear that it is sheep-shearing time. When your shepherds were with us, we did not ill-treat them, and the whole time they were with us nothing of theirs was missing. Ask your own servants and they will tell you. Therefore please be kind to my young men, and let them have any food that you can spare them."'

David's men went to Nabal and gave him David's message. Then they waited for his answer. They were in for a big surprise!

Nabal was rude and grumpy. He said to David's servants, 'Who is this David? Who is this son of Jesse? Why should I take my bread and water, and the meat I have prepared for my sheep shearers, and give it to men coming from who knows where? Be off with you!'

David's men turned round and went back. They told David everything Nabal had said. But then David made a big mistake. He decided to take revenge, and to have his own back. He said to his men, 'Put on your swords!' So they put them on, and David put on his. About four hundred men went up with David, while two hundred stayed behind. They were angry and furious because Nabal had been so unkind and unjust.

All would have gone sadly wrong if Mrs Peacemaker had not acted. One of Nabal's servants told his wife, Abigail, 'David sent messengers from the desert to give our master his greetings, but he insulted them. Yet David's men were very good to us. They did not ill-treat us when we were camped

near them. They were like a wall of protection all around us. Please see if you can do anything, because disaster is hanging over our master and all of us. He is such a wicked man that no-one can talk to him!'

Abigail decided at once what she must do. It required great courage, and she lost no time. She took two hundred loaves of bread, two barrels of wine, five roasted sheep, seventeen kilogrammes of roasted grain, bunches of raisins and two hundred cakes of dried figs, and loaded them on donkeys.

Then she told her servants, 'Go on ahead; I'll follow you.' She did not tell her husband what she was doing because she knew he would have said 'No' and caused an even greater fuss.

As she was riding her donkey round a bend on a hillside, she met David and his men coming towards her. David had just been saying to his men, 'Nabal has paid me back evil for the good I tried to do his men. We will kill every man in his camp by morning.'

Can you draw?

Draw Abigail meeting David, and include the donkeys carrying all the presents she took.

When Abigail saw David, she quickly got off her donkey and fell at his feet. She said, 'My lord, let the blame be on me alone. Please let your servant speak to you; hear what I have to say. Please pay no attention to what Nabal has said. I did not see the men you sent to my husband, otherwise I would have given them the food you need.'

She went on, 'I am glad that I have got to you in time before any fighting has begun. Please accept these gifts of food for the men who follow you. And please forgive my husband's behaviour, and do not have your own back. I know the Lord will fight for you, and give you success. Do not displease him.'

As David listened to her, he knew she was right. He had been so angry that he had not thought how silly his plan to have his own back was. He said to Abigail, 'Praise be to the Lord, who has sent you to meet me today. Thank God for your good sense and what you had done in stopping me from taking revenge.'

Then David accepted the gifts of food for his men, and said to Abigail, 'Go home in peace. I will do what you say.'

Abigail—Mrs Peacemaker—stopped David from taking revenge, which would have been a dreadful mistake. David knew he owed much to her, and he thanked God for her.

Abigail was right when she said that the Lord would fight for David against Nabal without David having to do anything. When Abigail returned home, Nabal was holding a party like that of a king. He was in high spirits and very drunk. So she told him nothing of what she had done until the morning. Then when he was sober, she told him everything, and the shock was so great that he had a stroke and was completely paralysed. He died ten days later.

How sad it would have been if David had gone against Nabal and killed him. He would then have been a murderer. The person who stopped him was Abigail, Mrs Peacemaker.

The Bible has many encouraging words for peacemakers. The Lord Jesus says to us, 'Blessed are the peacemakers, for they will be called sons of God.' The Lord Jesus Himself came to be a peacemaker. That is why he died on the Cross. We have made ourselves God's enemies by our sin and our disobedience to his commandments. But he loves us so much that he sent the Lord Jesus to be the peacemaker, the One who could bring us back to God. The cost was great. The Lord Jesus took the punishment for our sins—including sins like quarrelling and fighting, and the pride that is so often behind them. God wants us to put our trust in the Lord Jesus as our Saviour, and then to live our lives following him.

When the Lord Jesus is our Saviour, and we follow him, we learn how to become peacemakers.

The world needs peacemakers. Families need peacemakers too. When we see people we know well quarrelling or arguing, we should try to be peacemakers.

God gives wisdom to those who believe in Jesus when they ask him to make them peacemakers. Peacemakers please God, and they plant seeds of peace and reap a harvest of good things.

Where to read: 1 Samuel 25

Do you remember?

Saviour

A Saviour is someone who delivers or saves people from danger. It is a name especially given to the Lord Jesus because he died and rose again to save—or rescue—us from our sins and the death our sins deserve. His name 'Jesus' means 'God is the Saviour'.

Stop and think!

In which parts of the world are there wars and fighting today? Either now or when you go to bed tonight pray for peace, and for peacemakers too.

Miss Quizzer

Something to do

Mark the map!

Find where Sheba (modern Yemen) is on the map on page 123 and write in its name.

Do you like quizzes? Lots of people do. That is why there are so many quiz programmes on television and radio, and quiz books for sale in bookshops.

I want us to think about Miss Quizzer, the Queen who asked questions!

We do not know her name, except that she was the Queen of Sheba. She was the ruler of the Sabeans, a people who were very powerful from about 900 to 450 BC.

Today we would call her country the Yemen, and it is one of the hottest and driest parts of the world.

She had questions because of all she had heard about King Solomon. He was the third king of Israel, and the son of King David. He was known as the richest king in the world. Most nations knew too about the great Temple he had built for God, and about his successful navy and army.

But it was not these things that particularly interested the Queen of Sheba, Miss Quizzer. She had heard too of the great wisdom God had given him.

Solomon's wisdom was God's special gift to him. It had happened like this. Soon after Solomon took his father David's place as king, the Lord appeared to Solomon during the night in a dream, and said, 'Ask for whatever you want me to give you.'

Now Solomon could have asked to be wealthy

and famous, but instead he asked to be made wise so that he could govern God's people properly.

God was pleased with Solomon, and said to him, 'Since you have asked for this and not for long life or wealth for yourself, I will do what you have asked. I will make you wiser than anyone has ever been, and I will give you too what you have not asked for— riches and honour.'

God always keeps his promises, and he gave Solomon wisdom to make good laws. Solomon was able to decide whether something was good or bad, fair or unfair, right or wrong.

God gave him wisdom to build magnificent buildings, and to plant beautiful gardens and parks.

He was able to write poetry, and make up wise proverbs or sayings. There was no one as wise as Solomon in all the world!

When the Queen of Sheba heard about his wisdom, she did not believe anyone could be as wise as people said Solomon was. But the only way to find out the truth was to go and meet him, and ask him questions.

So off she went. It was a long journey on a camel of about 1,200 miles. As she travelled, she thought of all the hard questions she could ask Solomon. She probably asked some of the very wise and clever people of her own country to give her questions to ask. 'That question will beat him,' perhaps they said. 'Or if not that one, then this one will!'

Solomon made the Queen—Miss Quizzer—welcome when she arrived. She told him that she had heard about the wisdom God had given him, and she would like to ask him questions.

'Ask me whatever you would like to ask,' King Solomon said. And so she did! I expect she had a long list. But every question she asked, he answered perfectly. To even the most difficult questions, he knew the answers.

Lots of stories were told about Solomon's answers which are not in the Bible. We cannot be sure that they are true like the Bible, but they do show how everyone knew about Solomon's wisdom.

One story describes the final test the Queen made of Solomon's wisdom. Out in the palace garden she showed the king a bunch of the rarest and most beautiful flowers. They were not real flowers, but artificial ones. They were so cleverly made that by looking at them no one could tell the difference from real flowers.

Chapter 17

Although Solomon began well by asking God for wisdom, there came a time when he foolishly turned from God and worshipped idols. Perhaps he had become proud of his wisdom because of all the praise it brought him. But whatever the reason, turning away from God, he then spoiled the wonderful gift of wisdom God had given him, and he made sad mistakes in his life.

She deliberately did not let the king get close enough to smell them. She then asked him to tell her if they were real or artificial, not letting him hold them. I wonder what you would have done?

Some wild flowers were growing in the garden, and King Solomon said, 'Please put your bunch of flowers by those wild flowers.' And the queen did. The king had noticed a swarm of bees close by. They went to the wild flowers but none of the bees went near the artificial flowers because they could tell the difference!

'Your bunch of flowers is artificial,' said the King.

Miss Quizzer, the Queen of Sheba, was absolutely amazed at the King's wisdom. She said, 'The report I heard in my own country about your wisdom is true. I did not believe, but now I have seen it with my own eyes. The half was not told me. Praise be to the Lord your God who has placed you on the throne.'

Do you think anyone wiser than Solomon has lived in this world? Yes, the Lord Jesus Christ, God's Son.

People asked the Lord Jesus lots of questions. When the disciples did not understand the parables or stories Jesus told, they asked him questions, and he gave the answers.

Some people asked Jesus questions to try to catch him out, but they always failed. The Lord Jesus knew not only their questions, but what was going on in their minds and hearts.

You and I often have questions, and it is good to ask questions when we do not understand something.

I can think of lots of questions I have had. I wonder if you have had some of the same ones? Why is there wrong and evil in the world? How are we different from animals and other creatures? Why did God make us? Why did the Lord Jesus have to die upon the Cross if we were to be forgiven our sins?

Miss Quizzer—the Queen of Sheba—had to travel to the King's palace in Jerusalem to get her answers because God had given His wisdom to Solomon.

We do not have to travel a long way to find our answers. God has given us his Book, the Bible, which tells us about the life and teaching of the Lord Jesus, the one Person who can give answers to our most important questions.

The Bible promises that those who seek find. The Queen of Sheba really wanted to know the truth about Solomon's wisdom, and she found out the truth.

When we really want to find out the truth about the Lord Jesus from the Bible, we always discover it, and the Lord Jesus gives the right answers to the most important questions we ever ask.

Where to read: 1 Samuel 25; 1 Kings 10:1–13; 2 Chronicles 9:1–12

Did you know?

The Bible

The Bible is the world's best-selling book. The word 'Bible' comes from a Greek word meaning 'books', and the Bible contains 66 books. It is different from any other book because although lots of different people—probably as many as forty—wrote it, God made them want to write, and helped them so that all they wrote is true.

Mr Runaway

A runaway is someone who runs away from home, usually without telling anyone where he or she is going. I hope you have never thought of running away from home! Or perhaps from school! But if you ever have, I think I can guess what made you feel like it. It was probably when you did something wrong, and you were afraid of what might happen to you!

The person we are calling Mr. Runaway was a young man called Onesimus. Can you say that name? It is an unusual one, and it means 'useful'. That was a good name for him because he was a slave.

Slaves did not control their own lives, but instead belonged to other people, whom they called their 'masters'.

Unfortunately, slavery was common in the first century throughout the Roman empire.

People became slaves in different ways. Some were born slaves, because their parents were slaves.

Sometimes parents felt they could not look after their children when they were born, and they simply left them on the streets, and they were brought up slaves.

People who were poor even sold their children as slaves. Others became slaves to pay their debts. Some were kidnapped and then forced to be slaves.

We do not know how Onesimus became a slave,

but Roman laws gave his master great power over him. His master's name was Philemon and he lived in a place called Colosse.

Fortunately for Onesimus his master was a Christian. But that did not stop Onesimus running away.

Onesimus did something wrong. We do not know what it was, but it must have been something very bad.

Now when we do something bad, we usually deserve to get into trouble, don't we?

Onesimus decided to run away. It seems likely that he stole some of his master's possessions, perhaps to pay for the journey.

He travelled as fast as he could, and he made for a big city. It was either Ephesus or Rome. Ephesus was not far from Colosse, but it was large enough to get lost in. Rome was a much larger place—like London or New York—where many runaways went

because they thought they would be able to hide there.

Someone we know about was in prison in the city at the time—it was the apostle Paul. Paul was not a prisoner because of wrong he had done, but because some people did not want him to preach the good news about Jesus.

We do not know how Onesimus met Paul, but he did. Perhaps Onesimus was arrested, and found himself put in the same cell as Paul.

What do you think Paul wanted to talk about most of all with Onesimus? I am sure he wanted to tell him the good news about the Lord Jesus.

He said something like this to him, 'Onesimus, even though you have done wrong, God loves you. You have hurt not only your master, Philemon, but you have sinned against God. But the good news for you and me is that the Lord Jesus, God's Son, died for sinners, for people like us.'

Paul explained to Onesimus that he could be forgiven, if he was really sorry for what he had done, and put his trust in the Lord Jesus as his Saviour.

And that is just what Onesimus did! There in prison with Paul he received the Lord Jesus into his life as his Saviour, and all his sins were forgiven. How glad and grateful Onesimus was!

He then tried to help Paul in any way he could. He looked after him just as a son might care for his father. He became like his name—useful.

But one day Paul said, 'Onesimus, you must go back to your master. It is not right that you should look after me when you are really Philemon's slave.'

Onesimus was afraid about going back, because Philemon had great powers over him. Having run

Something to do

Mark the map!

Find where Rome, Ephesus and Colosse are on the map on page 123 and write in their names.

Paul's letters

In the Bible we have nine letters that Paul wrote to churches, and four that he wrote to individuals (two of them to the same person). Besides one letter to Philemon, he wrote to two other men, and both their names begin with the letter 'T'. Do you know who they were? They both come in the Bible just before the letter to Philemon.

away, he deserved even to be put to death according to Roman law.

Paul understood Onesimus' fears, and he also knew his master Philemon well. 'I'll write a letter for you,' Paul said. The letter went like this, 'I appeal to you for Onesimus, who has become a Christian, and like a son to me here in prison. Once he was useless to you, but now he has become useful both to you and to me. I am sending him back to you. I would have liked to keep him with me so that he could take your place in helping me while I am in prison. But I did not want to do anything without your permission. I did not want you to be kind because you had to but because you wanted to. Perhaps the reason he was separated from you for a little while was that you might have him back for good—no longer as a slave, but better than a slave, as a dear brother. He is very dear to me, but even dearer to you, both as a man and as a brother in the Lord. So if you consider me a friend, welcome him as you would welcome me. If he has done you any wrong or owes you anything, charge it to me.' That was a good letter for Onesimus to carry back to Colosse!

Onesimus had run away because he had done wrong, and was afraid.

He learned that it is impossible to run away from God because God is everywhere.

He discovered too that when we trust in the Lord Jesus as our Saviour, He teaches us not to run away from hard or difficult tasks and duties.

We may often be tempted to run away from something we ought to do. It is always silly, and it never works!

Sometimes people even try to run away from God! We cannot do that, because he sees and knows what we are doing wherever we are. If we try to run away from God, we run from the only One who can really help us. Onesimus discovered that.

God always helps runaways when they decide to do what is right. God gave Mr Runaway Paul's help, both in the prison and in the letter he wrote to Philemon for him.

When do you think Onesimus was happier—when he was running away from his master because he was afraid, or when he was going back to Colosse as a Christian with Paul's letter in his hand?

When we trust in the Lord Jesus, we discover we can be really happy only when we do what is right, and that is the lesson Mr Runaway, Onesimus, learned. It is an important lesson for us too. When we want to do the right thing the Lord Jesus is always with us to help us.

Where to read: Philemon 1–25

Mr Sulker

Something to do

Mark the map!

Find where Jezreel is on the map on page 122 and write in its name.

What do we mean when we say that people are sulking? We usually mean that they are cross and angry about something. When people sulk they may lose their temper or refuse to talk to anyone.

They may look sullen, miserable, cross and perhaps even pout. They may throw things on the ground or go into their bedroom and shut the door on everyone.

Have you seen anyone sulk? I wonder if you have ever sulked? It is not pleasant for other people when someone sulks. It usually makes others unhappy.

It is not only children who sulk, but grown up people too. The Bible tells about a king who sulked. His name was King Ahab. He was not a good king. Instead of worshipping the Lord Jehovah, the one true God, he worshipped false gods.

He foolishly married a wicked woman called Jezebel who encouraged him to worship her gods. He listened to her far more than he listened to God. God sent his prophet Elijah to tell Ahab what he ought to do, but he refused to listen.

King Ahab had a summer palace in Jezreel. One day he was looking out of his palace, and he noticed a fruitful vineyard nearby. It was close to a spring of water which kept everything green and attractive. He thought to himself, 'That would make a lovely vegetable garden.'

The vineyard belonged to a man called Naboth,

and the land had belonged to him, and his forefathers, for many many years.

King Ahab decided to speak to Naboth about it, and so he went to see him. He said, 'Let me have your vineyard to use for a vegetable garden, since it is close to my palace. In exchange I will give you a better vineyard or, if you prefer, I will pay you whatever it is worth.'

But Naboth knew he had to say 'no', and for a very good reason. 'I cannot let you have it,' replied Naboth, 'no matter how much you might be willing

to give me for it. This land is what the Lord gave to my father, and his father before him—and longer ago than that—and I must look after it, and leave it to my children when I die.'

That was a good and right reason for not wanting to sell the land.

Ahab was not at all pleased, and he showed it. He returned home, sullen and angry. He refused to talk to anyone, and went straight to his bedroom. He lay on his bed sulking and would not eat anything. And he was a king and a grown man!

Jezebel, his wife, found him, and asked, 'What on earth is wrong? Why aren't you eating? What has made you so angry and upset?'

'I asked Naboth to sell me his vineyard, or to exchange it for some other land, and he refused!' Ahab complained miserably.

'Is this how you act as a king?' asked Jezebel. 'Get up! Don't worry about it. You have something to eat, and I'll take care of Naboth and get you his vineyard.'

And she did! But she did something very nasty and wrong. She arranged for two men who would do anything bad if they were paid for it to accuse Naboth of cursing God and the king. That was a very serious crime. Of course, Naboth had done nothing of the sort, but the men in charge of the city of Jezreel did what Jezebel wanted, and they dragged Naboth out of the city and stoned him to death.

When Jezebel heard the news, she said to King Ahab, who was still sulking, 'Get up and take possession of Naboth's vineyard, which he refused to sell you. He is no longer alive, but dead.'

Instead of asking what had happened to Naboth

or being sad that Naboth had died, King Ahab got up and went down to take possession of Naboth's vineyard. He was not sulking any more, now he was pleased.

But God was not pleased. Soon God sent his prophet Elijah to Ahab to tell him that he knew all about his sulking and what had happened to Naboth.

God does not like us sulking because sulking means we are thinking of ourselves rather than others—and that is selfishness. God does not like sulking because it often shows that we are not happy with what we already have.

But most of all he does not like sulking because it is the opposite of our being like the Lord Jesus Christ.

Place a 'T' where true, and 'F' where false against these sentences:

When we sulk we are happy.

When we sulk we look miserable.

When we sulk people like to be with us.

When we sulk we are thinking of ourselves rather than others.

We do not please God when we sulk.

The Lord Jesus never sulked; instead, he was always kind, loving, pleasant and unselfish, and that is what God wants us to be like. When we trust the Lord Jesus as our Saviour, and he lives in us by his Spirit, he teaches us not to sulk.

Do we sulk? If we do, is it because we do not know the Lord Jesus as our Saviour? Or is it because we are not listening to God's Spirit when he tells us that he wants us to be like Jesus?

When we are tempted to sulk we should remember the bad example of King Ahab—Mr Sulker—and the horrible effects it had on others.

Where to read: 1 Kings 21:1–19

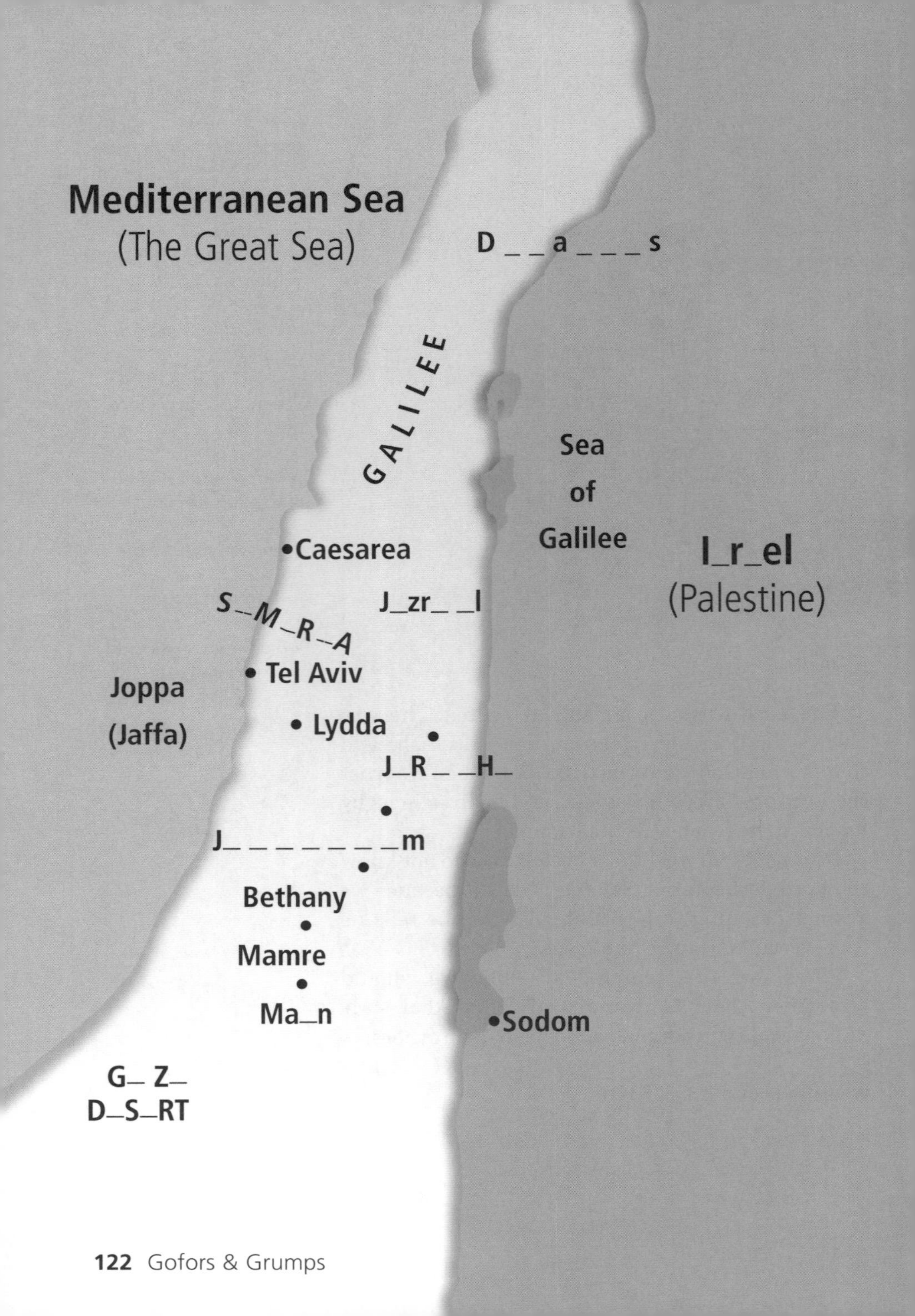

Mediterranean Sea
(The Great Sea)

D _ _ a _ _ _ s

GALILEE

Sea
of
Galilee

I_r_el
(Palestine)

•Caesarea

J_zr_ _l

S _ M _ R _ A

• Tel Aviv

Joppa

(Jaffa)

• Lydda

•

J_R_ _H_

•

J_ _ _ _ _ _ _m

•

Bethany

•

Mamre

•

Ma_n

•Sodom

G_ Z_
D_S_RT

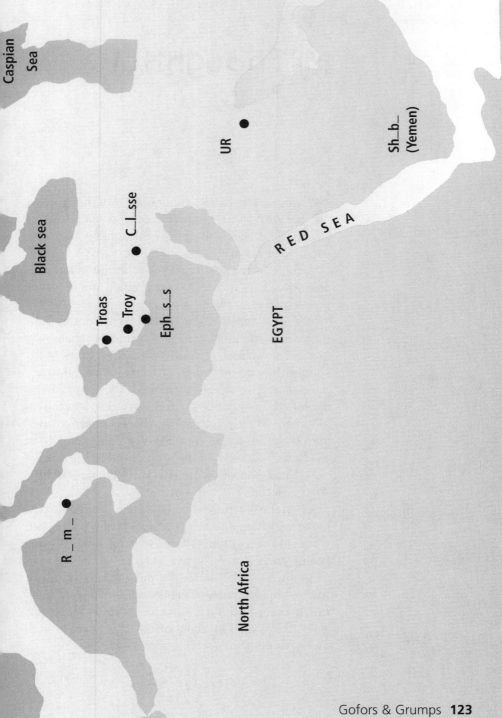

Caspian
Sea

Black sea

Troas

Troy

C_l_sse

Eph_s_s

UR

Sh_b_
(Yemen)

RED SEA

EGYPT

R_m_

North Africa

MrThoughtful

I wonder if you are a thoughtful or a thoughtless person? A thoughtful person is 'full of thought', someone who thinks of how he or she can help or serve others.

A thoughtless person on the other hand is someone who does not think very much about other people and their feelings.

A school teacher told her class to notice how many bad spellings they could find on their way home from school. Opposite the school there was a shop with prices of things written on its windows.

As soon as the girls looked they saw many mistakes. They sat down and started writing them all down. They giggled. 'Oh, there's another one,' and they laughed triumphantly, 'only one l, in woollens.' 'Look how he's spelt cardigan with a "k"!' 'And trousers with two "o"s.' They thought it was great fun.

Then the old man who owned the shop came out, looked at them and at the shop window and asked what they were doing. 'We're writing down all your spelling mistakes—the teacher told us.'

There was silence. He did not chase them away. Instead his face turned crimson, and he went back into his shop without a word. The girls suddenly felt sick—they had been thoughtless. It is never kind to make fun of other people's mistakes.

Something to do

Mark the map!

Find where Ephesus and Rome are on the map on page 167 and write in their names.

I wonder if you and I are ever thoughtless? Let me tell you about Mr Thoughtful, whose real name was Onesiphorus.

He lived at one time in Ephesus, the most important city in the Roman province of Asia, on the west coast of what is now Asiatic Turkey.

The apostle Paul stayed for a while in Ephesus too, and it was here that he first met Onesiphorus.

Later on Paul was put in prison in Rome—the capital of the Roman Empire. And who do you think came to visit him? Yes, Mr Thoughtful or Onesiphorus.

Onesiphorus heard that Paul was a prisoner, and he was concerned about him. He thought, 'Paul must be very lonely, and I am sure that he would love a visit from a friend. He would like news too of his other friends in Ephesus. Perhaps he needs money, or food, or clothes or books. I know what I'll do, I'll find out where Paul is and I'll visit him.'

Now that was not as easy as it may sound.

Onesiphorus may not have been to Rome before, and it was a huge city, in which a person could easily get lost. Also about this time, there had been a fire, and many things in the city had changed.

Nevertheless, Onesiphorus went. He searched hard until he found where Paul was. He may have had great difficulty in getting permission to see him, but he managed it. It may have been dangerous because he was letting people know that he was a Christian too, like Paul. But still he went. He was not ashamed that Paul was a prisoner, or what people may have thought about him for visiting someone who was a prisoner.

Paul was surprised and pleased to see him! It was not just because of the books, or the food, or the warm clothes, or the money he brought. It was because Onesiphorus's thoughtfulness showed that he really cared about Paul.

Thoughtful people think about others. Thoughtful people often do kind things people do not expect. Thoughtful people go to a lot of trouble

In what ways can we be thoughtful for others? What kind and helpful things can we do for our family and for our friends? Will you try to be thoughtful? As important as our trying to be thoughtful is our asking the Lord Jesus to help us.

to help others. When your mother is tired, are you thoughtful when you see a big pile of washing up in the kitchen sink?

A girl called Helen went to university. As a new student she felt very nervous and home-sick on her first day as she unpacked her things. She went to look in her mirror, and someone had written across her mirror, 'If you don't know anyone, and have nowhere to go after supper, come and have coffee in my room, number 12, at 8 pm.' It was signed 'Dorothy'. Helen's eyes blurred, and a lump filled her throat. Helen met Dorothy and discovered that she was a Christian, and a thoughtful Christian.

Christians ought to be thoughtful, because God, their Heavenly Father, is thoughtful.

The Lord Jesus, God's Son and our Saviour, showed in lots of ways how thoughtful God is. A little girl, the daughter of Jairus, died, and the Lord Jesus brought her back to life again. All the people were pleased and excited, but they all forgot something very important! But not the Lord Jesus, because he was always thoughtful. He said to them, 'Give her something to eat!' They had all forgotten that she would be hungry, as boys and girls usually are!

Even when the Lord Jesus was dying on the Cross, he was thoughtful. His mother was standing near the Cross with John, one of his disciples. He said to John, 'Look after her, please, John, as you would your own mother.'

When we become Christians, the Lord Jesus lives within us by his Spirit, and his Spirit teaches us to be thoughtful for others.

Where to read: 2 Timothy 1:16–18

Miss Useful

Do you remember?

Saviour

A Saviour is someone who delivers or saves people from danger. It is a name especially given to the Lord Jesus because he died and rose again to save—or rescue—us from our sins and the death our sins deserve. His name 'Jesus' means 'God is the Saviour'.

Do you know what a paper-knife is? It is a kind of knife—although not always made of metal—which we use especially for opening envelopes and letters. I have two but one does a better job than the other. One is slender and sharp, and the other is thick and blunt.

One is useful, and the other is almost useless. That is rather like our lives: they may either be useful to God and to others, or they may be of little use, and, sadly, even useless.

God wants us to be useful to him and to other people. When we trust the Lord Jesus as our Saviour, God's purpose is always to make us useful. He gives us gifts and abilities with which we can serve others and please him.

In the Bible God has given us lots of examples of people who were useful. We are going to think about one of them. Miss Useful's real name was Rhoda.

She lived in Jerusalem, and helped in the home of Mary, the mother of John Mark, who wrote one of the books in the Bible which tells us the good news about the Lord Jesus.

Mary was probably a widow. She needed help in the house because it was rather large, and was one of the regular meeting places for Christians in Jerusalem. Christians often met there to pray together.

Rhoda did jobs about the house. She probably did some of the shopping, helped with the dishes, and the washing and mending of clothes.

But something dreadful happened! King Herod arrested some of the Jerusalem Christians, and he made life very difficult for them.

He had James, the brother of John, put to death with the sword. When he saw that this pleased the Jews, he decided to seize Peter too.

After arresting Peter, he put him in prison, handing him over to be guarded by four squads of soldiers.

The Christians in Jerusalem decided there was only one thing they could do, and that was to meet together to pray for Peter.

One of the places they met was Mary's home. Lots of people came to pray. As they knocked at the door, they had to be let in, and someone was needed to look after that. Who do you think had that task? Yes, Rhoda, or Miss Useful.

Backwards and forwards she ran, opening the door and letting people in to join the prayer meeting.

'Lord, please save Peter,' they must have prayed. And perhaps John Mark, who may already have started writing his gospel, prayed, 'Please keep Peter safe so that he can help me write about the Lord Jesus.'

God always answers our prayers, although not always in the way we expect. As the Christians prayed together in Mary's house, they did not know that Peter was fast asleep in the prison, bound with two chains, with sentries standing guard at the entrance.

Suddenly an angel of the Lord appeared and a

Our Bible dictionary

The gospels

The word 'gospel' means 'good news', and is a special word for the good news about the Lord Jesus. But it is also the word used to describe the four books in the Bible—by Matthew, Mark, Luke and John—which tell us the good news about the Lord Jesus' life, teaching, death and resurrection. They were written to help us understand that the Lord Jesus is God's Son, so that we might believe in him and become God's children.

light shone in the cell. He struck Peter on the side and woke him up. 'Quick, get up!' he said. Peter's chains fell off his wrists.

Then the angel said to him, 'Put on your clothes and sandals.' And Peter did so. 'Wrap your cloak around you and follow me,' the angel told him.

Peter followed him out of the prison, but he had no idea that what the angel was doing was really happening. He thought he was seeing a vision or having a dream.

They passed through the first and second guards and came to the iron gate leading to the city. It opened for them by itself, and they went through it. When they had walked the length of one street, the angel suddenly left him.

Then Peter realized what had happened and he said, 'Now I know without a doubt that the Lord sent his angel and rescued me from Herod's

Chapter 21

Can you draw some pictures—perhaps like a cartoon strip—of Peter's escape from prison and the Christians praying for his release? Do not forget to include Rhoda!

clutches and from everything the Jewish people were hoping to do to me.'

Now there was one place he had to go to straightaway. Can you guess where it was? Yes, it was Mary's house, for Peter knew or guessed that Christians would be there praying for him.

He arrived at the house, and knocked at the outer entrance. And, of course, it was Rhoda who went to the door. She had been taught to ask, 'Who is it?' because with Christians in danger, she was only to let in those who were friends.

'Who is it?' Rhoda asked. 'It's Peter!' he replied. When Rhoda recognised Peter's voice, she was so excited and glad that without opening the door to Peter she ran back to where all the Christians were, and shouted, 'Peter is at the door!'

'You are out of your mind,' they told her. When she kept on insisting that it was so, they said, 'It must be his angel.'

But Peter kept on knocking! When they opened the door and saw him, they were astonished. Peter signalled them to be quiet and he described how the Lord had brought him out of prison.

Rhoda had been the first to know the good news! And she believed it to be Peter when others doubted. Of course, she had not been useful in opening the door to him at first, but then she had been so excited!

Even though Rhoda was only a young girl, she was useful to others, and useful in opening the door for people.

What Rhoda did saved others, who were busy, from being disturbed. What Rhoda did, though a small thing, was important.

Her faithfulness in small things must have led to

greater responsibilities as she grew older. The fact that her name is mentioned in the Bible—remember she was only a servant-girl—probably means she became well-known among Christians in Jerusalem.

Although what Rhoda did was small, she pleased God by her faith. She had not doubted that it was Peter at the door.

When we love the Lord Jesus, we want to be useful to him. I remember when a friend of mine, a postman, became a Christian. We wanted someone to fix small plastic holders in front of every seat in the church, in which we could put a welcome card for visitors. It was going to take hours and hours to do, and it was a really boring task. But my friend was so grateful to the Lord Jesus for dying for him, and forgiving him his sins, nothing was too much trouble for him! He became Mr Useful. Like Rhoda, as he became useful in small things, God gave him larger things to do.

Are we useful or useless when it comes to helping and serving? If the Lord Jesus has forgiven us our sins, we will be so grateful to him that nothing will be too much trouble if we know it is what he wants us to do. That will make us useful to God and to others.

Where to read: Acts 12:1–19

Mr Violent

Have you ever lost your temper, and then said and done things you have been sorry about afterwards? Most, if not all of us have done that sometimes. Things are made worse if we are then violent, and perhaps hit out at other people.

Violence can happen very quickly if we lose our temper and do not think what we are doing. Violence is always nasty, and there is seldom an excuse for it.

People are sometimes violent in sport, and it always spoils the sport, whether it is football, rugby, cricket or any other game.

When people get drunk, they may become violent, and that is a good reason for not drinking alcohol or spirits because they take away our power to control ourselves.

Parents may sometimes make the mistake of being violent in punishing their children; and children may be violent by kicking and punching. In schools there may be bullies who like hurting other boys and girls.

A lot of violence is shown on television, and people make video nasties which are just full of it. It is not good to look at violence on television or in films because what we watch influences the way we behave.

Our Bible dictionary

Christ or Messiah

'Christ' and 'Messiah' mean the same thing—'The Anointed One'. To 'anoint' people is to pour oil on their heads, usually as a sign to show that they have been especially chosen for a task. Kings and queens are often anointed when they are crowned. The name 'Christ' or 'Messiah' is given to the Lord Jesus because God especially chose him to be the one who would die to be the Saviour of his people.

Unfortunately it is possible to love violence, and to like being cruel. The Bible tells us not to envy violent people or choose any of their ways because it will lead us down a wrong path. God hates violence.

Several people in the Bible might be called Mr Violent, but I have chosen Saul, or Paul as we usually call him. Saul was his Jewish name, and Paul his Roman name. We will call him Paul from now on.

He lived in the first century, and was a very religious Jew. Like all Jews, he was waiting for the Messiah, the Christ, to come. But he did not understand properly God's promises in the first half of the Bible, what we call the Old Testament, about the Messiah. He expected him to come as a mighty King and to be someone whom everyone would immediately worship and obey.

The Lord Jesus is the Messiah, the Christ, whom God promised. When he came into the world, he lived a perfect life. He taught as no one had ever taught before. And then after three years of teaching and doing good, he died on the Cross to save us from our sins, according to God's plan. Three days after, he rose again. He had overcome sin, death, and Satan. The disciples could not have been more excited, and they went everywhere telling everyone.

But Paul did not believe what they said. He did not think that the Messiah he waited for would die on a Cross like a common criminal. Of course, Paul was wrong, but he did not understand this.

When he heard Jesus' followers telling everyone the good news that Jesus had died, and then risen again to make it possible for us to be forgiven and to become God's children, Paul was angry, and said, 'It's not true!'

He was so filled with hatred for Christians that he tried to do them harm. He got permission from the Jewish rulers to have them arrested. He was violent to Christians in and near Jerusalem. He was cruel because he foolishly thought he was serving God by hurting them.

Christians knew their lives were in danger because of Paul. Many of them must have prayed for him.

I am glad to tell you that Paul stopped being violent after something wonderful happened in his life—something that has happened to many other people.

Mr Violent met the one person who could change him. He met Jesus!

Paul had decided to go to Damascus to do to the Christians there what he had done in Jerusalem. He wanted to arrest them, and bring them in chains to Jerusalem.

As he was getting close to Damascus, a bright

Do you remember?

Jerusalem

Jerusalem is one of the oldest cities in the world. King David made it his capital city, and his son Solomon built God's House— the Temple—there. It is very high up in the hills, and the ground slopes away steeply on three of its sides. That is why people are said to 'go up' to Jerusalem or 'down' from it. The Lord Jesus was often in Jerusalem, and it was outside the walls of the city that he was put to death.

light suddenly flashed around him. He fell to the ground and he heard a voice, 'Paul! Paul! Why are you persecuting me?' 'Who are you, Lord?' Paul asked. 'I am Jesus, whom you are persecuting! Now get up and go into the city and I will tell you what you are to do.'

Paul knew now that he had been dreadfully

wrong about Jesus. Jesus really is the Son of God, and he is alive from the dead!

Paul understood then that he had been wrong about Christians too; and he had been wrong to use violence. There and then he confessed his sins, and the Lord Jesus forgave him, and made him one of his followers.

Paul never forgot how foolish he had once been about Jesus, and about violence. He immediately told everyone he could that Jesus is the Christ, the Son of God. He spent the rest of his life serving him and others.

Have you and I been violent? If so, we ought to be ashamed, and remember how much God hates violence. But just as the Lord Jesus forgave Paul when he realised how wrong he had been, the Lord Jesus will forgive us.

When we trust the Lord Jesus as our Saviour, he teaches us not to be violent, but self-controlled and kind. He helps us to be like him. When people were violent against the Lord Jesus, he did not answer back with violence, but, instead, he prayed for them.

The secret of the change in our behaviour when we become Christians is that the Lord Jesus comes to live within us by his Spirit. His Spirit gives us strength to be like Jesus, and to want to do only what is kind to others.

Where to read: Acts 26:9–18

Look up too: Proverbs 3:31; Proverbs 16:29 and 1 Timothy 1:13-15.

Something to do

Mark the map!

Find where Damascus is on the map on page 166 and write in its name.

Mr Walk-with-God

Mr Walk-with-God was someone special, because he was one of the first people to love having God as his friend. He deserves a place in any book of records. He lived in the earliest period of human history. His name was Enoch, and his great-great-great-great grandfather was Adam.

The most important thing we know about Enoch was that he walked with God. We are going to have to do some detective work to understand what the Bible means when it tells us that he walked with God but it will not be too difficult.

You often walk with other people, perhaps your Mum or Dad, or a friend. When you walk with them, you keep close to them. Enoch kept close to God, which means that he talked to God in prayer, and he gave time to God in his life.

To walk with people we keep in step with them. Enoch walked in step with God because he obeyed God. If we really want to walk with someone, we let him or her choose the way, and we follow. Enoch wanted God to choose the way he should go.

Enoch enjoyed having God as his friend, and it changed his whole life so that he became more and more like God in the way he behaved and the kind of person he was. Have you noticed how friends become like one another?

When we walk with God, his Spirit makes us more and more like him, because we want to do what is right, and be helpful to others.

Enoch can be called Mr Walk-with-God because he was unusual. Most other people did not walk with God. Enoch stood out because lots of other people did not even believe that God exists. Enoch not only believed God exists, but he believed that God rewards those who sincerely seek him. And he was right!

But that did not make life easy for Enoch. He

made a choice that others were not willing to make. He walked with God when others did not. He was not afraid of being different.

Do you like being different from others? I expect not. Even with things like clothes and shoes we do not like being different from others in case people think us strange. When we go shopping for clothes we may say, 'I want that because others at school are wearing things like it.'

Enoch was willing to go against the flow of the crowd. Have you ever walked in the opposite direction to a large number of people? Perhaps you have been to a football match or a concert, and as you have begun to leave, you have remembered that you have left something behind. You have then had to go all the way back to get it, and instead of going easily in the direction of the crowd, you have gone with great difficulty in the opposite way. It is not easy! It was a bit like that for Enoch.

People probably made fun of Enoch, but he took no notice. We may think him brave; and he was. But the secret of his strength was his friendship with God.

Enoch had not always walked with God. It is here that we must do a little detective work again. How or when did he become Mr Walk-with-God? There is just a hint in the Bible that it was the birth of his son, Methuselah, that made Enoch first think of walking with God. Perhaps it was a difficult birth, and Enoch cried to God to help his wife and baby son. Maybe he was just filled with amazement at the wonderful gift of life in a new baby.

Enoch lived many years of his life walking out of step with God, but that all changed one day. No one is born into this world walking with God. We all

Something to do

Ask your parents how they felt when you were born. I would not be surprised if they felt like Enoch!

begin our lives out of step with him. That is why the Lord Jesus came into the world two thousand years ago. He came to die upon the Cross for sinners like us who have failed to walk in God's ways. When we are sorry for our sins, and trust in him as our

Heaven

Heaven is where God lives. The Lord Jesus came from heaven, and returned there when his work on earth was done. It is from heaven that the Lord Jesus will come when he returns. For those who trust in the Lord Jesus it is their heavenly Father's House and their home, where one day they are going to live for ever. No one deserves to go to heaven. The only way to heaven is through trusting in the Lord Jesus as our Saviour.

Saviour, he teaches us then to walk with God. He gives us his own example to follow, and his Spirit to live within our hearts to make us strong and courageous.

We said that Enoch was special, and deserved to be in a book of records, because he is the first person in the Bible whose special friendship with God is mentioned. But there is another reason why he was special. He is the first person who went to heaven without dying!

The Bible says that one day Enoch simply disappeared, because God took him! A girl in Sunday School put it like this: 'One day Enoch and God went out for a walk together and they got so far from Enoch's home that God said to him, "We're nearer my home than yours, why don't you come to tea?" And he did!

I do not know exactly what happened, but I know it was very wonderful for Enoch! Enoch loved God so much that nothing was better for Enoch than being with God for ever.

God has a place in heaven for everyone who walks with him on earth.

I wonder if we are walking with God? Have we begun to walk with him yet? The place to begin is to be sorry for not walking with him, and to ask the Lord Jesus to be our Saviour. Then he gives us strength to walk with God.

Where to read: Genesis 5:18–24; Hebrews 11:1–6

Chapter 24

Mr X-Ray

Xis probably the most difficult letter in the alphabet for which to find a Bible character! But I have thought of someone whom we may call Mr X-Ray.

An X-Ray is the name given to an important discovery in 1896 by a Professor called Röntgen. He used the letter 'X' to indicate that neither he nor anyone else could understand how these invisible rays worked, but they did understand what X-Rays could do. 'X' stood for something they were sure of, but which they could not explain. So they called the rays they discovered X-Rays.

Security officers at airports X-Ray people's

belongings. They use X-Ray machines to search for illegal goods such as bombs or drugs. Each piece of luggage is X-Rayed before being loaded on board a plane.

Every day of the week in hospitals around the world people have X-Rays. They provide a special photograph of our bodies so that doctors can see if there is anything wrong.

Have you ever had an X-Ray? If we break an arm or a leg, doctors will want us to have an X-Ray before they try to put things straight.

An X-Ray is a way of seeing things which would otherwise be hidden or secret. That is why I am calling the apostle Peter Mr X-Ray.

Let me tell what happened. In the early days of the Church in Jerusalem, many people became Christians, and some were poor and others were better off and even rich. Those who believed in the

Do you remember?

Apostles

An apostle is someone sent out as a messenger. Although it can mean any sort of messenger, it describes the men the Lord Jesus first chose to be his special followers so that they might be eye-witnesses of his life and work, and especially of his resurrection.

Do you remember?

Jerusalem

See page 139.

Lord Jesus shared everything with each other, and cared for one another.

No one was allowed to be poor because many who owned land or houses sold them, or part of them, and brought the money to the apostles for them to give to people in need. It was a kind and generous thing to do.

But here we come to the sad part of the story. A husband and wife did a silly thing. A man called Ananias decided to sell a property that he had, and to give some of the money he got for it to the poor. But when he brought the money to the apostles, he pretended that it was all the money he had received. Sapphira, his wife, agreed with what he did.

It was a foolish idea. Ananias and Sapphira did not need to give all the money from their property to God for his people. But they wanted others to think them more generous than they were. They were deceitful. They were really telling a lie.

But they had forgotten something important. God sees and knows everything! He can see what no one else can see. He can 'X-Ray' our minds and hearts, even better than doctors can X-Ray our bodies.

Ananias and Sapphira had also forgotten something else. God gives his Holy Spirit to those who trust the Lord Jesus as their Saviour, and obey him. God's Spirit lived in Peter and the other apostles, to whom Ananias brought his gift of money for God.

As soon as Ananias came with the money, Peter knew something was wrong. He was filled with the Holy Spirit and he saw through Ananias' deceit. God gave Peter X-Ray eyes so that he saw what ordinary eyes could not see.

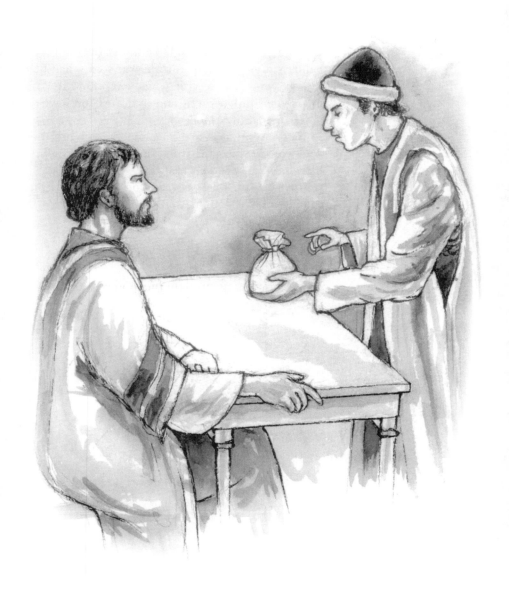

Peter said, 'Ananias, how is it that Satan has so filled your heart that you have lied to the Holy Spirit and have kept for yourself some of the money you received for the land? Didn't it belong to you before it was sold? And after it was sold, wasn't the money yours to do with what you wanted? What made you think of doing such a thing? You have not lied to men, but to God.'

When Ananias heard this, he fell down and died. And exactly the same thing happened to Sapphira, his wife.

It was because Peter was filled with God's Spirit that he saw through Ananias and Sapphira's lie,

and knew what Satan had put into their hearts to do. Peter was Mr X-Ray because he was filled with the Holy Spirit.

It is always good to remember that God sees what no one else can see. He knows all our thoughts. He knows what we are going to say even before we say it!

God also helps his servants to see what cannot be seen by the human eye when it is important for them to do so. We call this insight. It is a gift God gives by his Spirit.

We can never deceive God. We often cannot deceive those in whom God's Spirit lives.

One of the most wonderful things about being a Christian is that God's Holy Spirit comes to live within us. He helps us to see and understand things we would not otherwise be able to see and understand. Most of all he helps us to understand the Bible, and to know that the Lord Jesus is always near to help us.

If only Ananias and Sapphira had really trusted the Lord Jesus as their Saviour, and allowed his Spirit to fill their lives! Then—like Peter—they would have known that possessing the Lord Jesus is much more valuable and precious than any piece of land or property! The Holy Spirit is a wonderful gift to every Christian from our heavenly Father and our Saviour, the Lord Jesus.

Where to read: Acts 4:32–5:10

Our Bible dictionary

The Holy Spirit

There is only one true God, and he is one in three distinct Persons, Father, Son and Holy Spirit.

The Holy Spirit is God, and he is the Third Person of the Trinity. The Trinity—three in unity—is the name we give to this special oneness that God has in Three Persons.

It is not easy for us to understand, but we must remember that we are talking about God who is very great, and our minds are much too small to understand everything about him.

The Holy Spirit has given us the Bible because he prompted the writers to write, and made sure that they wrote only what is true.

Mr Yawner

Something to do

Mark the map!
Find again where Troas and Troy are on the map on page 167.

What does it mean to yawn? When we yawn we open our mouth wide to draw in air. It shows we are either tired or bored! See if you can do a yawn! That now makes us all like Mr Yawner whom we are going to think about!

Mr Yawner was a young man, and his real name was Eutychus. In his own Greek language, his name meant 'Lucky'.

He lived in a city called Troas, near the old city of Troy. It was a Roman colony, and was the port for travellers from Asia to Europe.

Paul visited Troas for a week. His last day there was a Sunday.

Why is Sunday so important to Christians? Yes, because it is in a special way God's Day. Saturday is the day the Jews kept special to remember how in the beginning God made everything in six days and how that then he rested on the seventh day. But Christians keep the first day of the week— Sunday—special because it was on the first day of the week that the Lord Jesus rose again from the dead. So on Sundays we remember that God made the world and, second, that the Lord Jesus rose again and lives today—and forever!

In Troas all the Christians met together on a Sunday to worship God. But they were not able to do this as easily as we do.

A Christian

People who believe in the Lord Jesus were first called Christians as a nick-name. Christians are those who belong to the Lord Jesus because they know that he died for their sins and rose again to be their Saviour and Lord. It is another name for those who follow the Lord Jesus.

Many of them were slaves. That meant that they had to work hard all day, and every day, and they could only meet to worship God with other Christians when their daily work was done.

They did not have church buildings like most of us, but they met in an upstairs room, on the third floor. Perhaps you live in a block of flats with several floors or your school has more than one storey.

The Christians met together first to remember the Lord Jesus in what we call the Lord's Supper or the Communion Service. And then they listened to God's Word being taught and preached.

On this occasion when Paul was there, he preached. As he was leaving the next day, there was a lot he wanted to talk to them about.

And so he preached a long time! For lights, they had oil lamps. They not only gave light, but they gave off heat.

The room grew hotter and hotter. The flickering lamps and warm atmosphere caused by all the people being squashed into one room made it difficult to keep awake, and especially for those who had been working hard all day.

Eutychus was probably already tired when he arrived, but he wanted to hear God's Word. He went and sat in the window. As the room became warmer and warmer, Eutychus's eyes began to close, and his head began to fall—and then he jerked himself up to try to keep awake. But soon he fell asleep again.

And then something dreadful happened! He fell out of the window down into the street below. When everyone ran down to see if they could help him, they found that he was dead.

Paul went down too. He took the young man up

into his arms. Then a miracle took place! Paul said, 'Don't be alarmed. He is alive!'

How pleased and delighted all the Christians were! Paul then carried on preaching!

What do we learn from Eutychus, Mr Yawner? Never sit in a window, especially if it is above the first floor!

Do you remember?

The Lord's Supper

At the Lord's Supper Christians eat bread and drink wine, as the first disciples did on the night the Lord Jesus was betrayed. The bread and the wine are symbols or pictures of the Lord Jesus' body and blood. Another name for the Lord's Supper is the Communion Service— 'communion' means fellowship or sharing. At the Lord's Supper Christians remember with gratitude how they share in the wonderful benefits that come to them through the Lord Jesus' death for them—especially the forgiveness of sins. They also look forward to the time when the Lord Jesus comes again to take all his people to be with him for ever.

But there are other important lessons. It is a great gift and privilege to be able to have Sundays free from school and work so that we can join with others to worship God and hear his Word.

No matter how busy we are, we should always meet with God's people on his Day.

Eutychus probably could not help yawning. But we often can help it, can't we? The best preparation for Sunday is an early night to bed on a Saturday. Sometimes we cannot help being Master or Miss

Yawner because we have had to be up late for some good reason. But let us try to make sure that it is not our fault!

Where to read: Acts 20:6–12

Mr Zoo-keeper

There is really no doubt about whom we may call Mr Zoo-keeper in the Bible. It is Noah who built an ark for the animals and his family.

The word 'zoo' comes from the first three letters of the word 'zoological'.

Zoologists is the name given to scientists who study animals, and care about them.

Noah cared very much about the animals he took into his large wooden boat. But behind his care of the animals, there was a very sad story. The wickedness of men and women in the world had become great, and was getting worse and worse.

God decided to punish the world with a flood. But there was one man who really did trust in God and who wanted to please him, and that was Noah.

God decided to save Noah and his family, together with some of every kind of bird and animal so that there might be a new beginning for the world.

God told Noah how to build a great boat, called an ark. It was 450 feet long, 75 feet wide and 45 feet high.

God told Noah to take two of all living creatures, male and female, to keep them alive with him, whether they were birds that flew or animals that moved along the ground. Some kinds of animal God

Can you draw?

Draw an ark with Noah, his family, and the animals going into it.

chose for Noah and his family and the animals to eat, and so God told him to take more of each of these.

As well as that, he had to collect and store away every kind of food for each of them. What a job!

The flood came just as God promised. Noah, and his family, and all the animals in the ark, were kept safe.

God judged the world in such a serious way because of the bad things that men and women did. Their sin brought harm to the animals and birds as well as to boys and girls, and men and women.

That is true today, isn't it? When we pollute the atmosphere, spoil the countryside, we bring harm

to God's creatures. That is why some birds and animals are now extinct.

God chose Noah to be Mr Zoo-keeper to show us that he cares about animals. He told Noah to take the right food for each of them.

We too ought to care for all God's creatures.

We should think about them, just as God thought about not only Noah in the ark, but the birds and animals too.

It is thoughtful to feed the birds in winter, and to keep our animals indoors when events like firework displays are taking place.

Noah was Mr Zoo-keeper because God knew that we need animals. We need some for the help they give us, and others for food.

Animals are often company for people. Our pets become good friends. Animals also provide us with food to eat.

Noah was Mr Zoo-keeper too because God used certain animals as pictures of the Lord Jesus. Some of the extra animals Noah took into the ark he offered as a sacrifice when he came out of it.

The death of those animals could never take away sins, but it was God's way of preparing the world for the coming of the Lord Jesus, the Lamb of God, who can take away our sins.

Did you know?

The rainbow

Do you know what we are meant to remember every time we see a rainbow? Look up what God said to Noah and his sons in Genesis 9:8–17.

Something to do

Make a short list of some pets who can be good company

1.

2.

3.

So there are helpful lessons we learn from Noah, Mr Zoo-keeper.

Whenever we see wild animals, who make us afraid, we should remember that it was human sin in the beginning that made them like that. Adam and Eve's sin spoiled the whole of God's creation.

We should care about animals, and look after them. God does, and he wants us to share his care.

And, most of all, we should thank God for the Lord Jesus, the Lamb of God, for whose coming even Noah prepared the way as he took animals like sheep and lambs into the ark.

Where to read: Genesis 6:5–22

Mediterranean Sea
(The Great Sea)

D_M_S_ _S

GALILEE

Sea
of
Galilee

Israel
(Palestine)

SAMARIA

•Caesarea

Jezreel

• Tel Aviv

Joppa
(Jaffa)

• Lydda

•
Jericho

•

Jerusalem

•

Bethany
•

Mamre
•

Maon

•Sodom

GAZA
DESERT

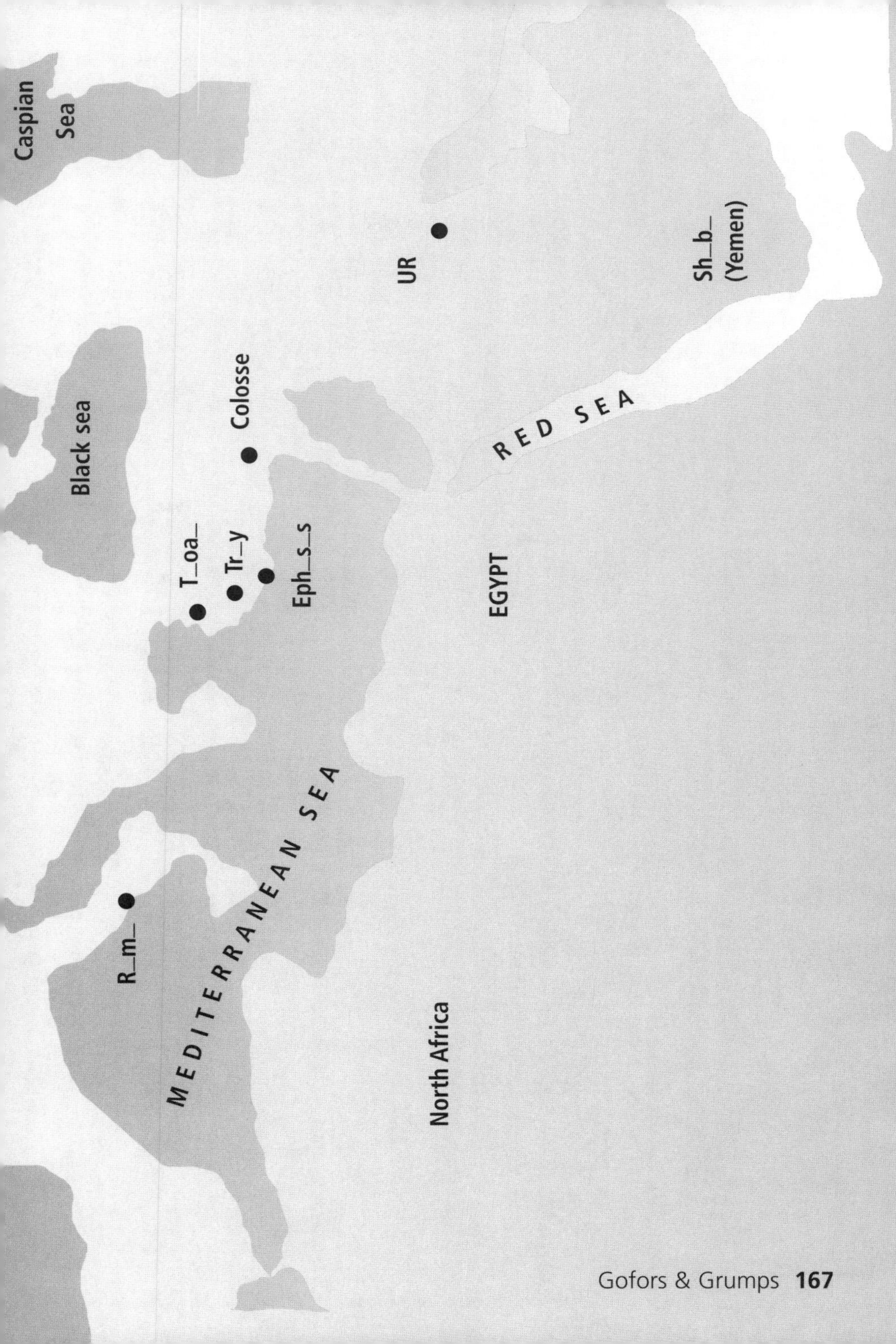

Caspian Sea

Black sea

Colosse

T_oa_

Tr_y

Eph_s_s

UR

Sh_b_
(Yemen)

RED SEA

EGYPT

R_m_

MEDITERRANEAN SEA

North Africa

Other books for children

 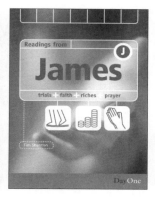 

THE LIFE OF ABRAHAM

A BOOK OF READINGS BASED
ON THE LIFE OF ABRAHAM

TIM SHENTON

Does God answer prayer?
What are the promises of
God? How can we deal with
temptation? These are some
of the subjects answered in
this study guide for the young.
Full of interesting stories and
examples that younger
readers can relate to in their
own lives, each chapter in this
book ends with points for
thought and prayer, making it
a superb tool for enriching the
spiritual lives of young people.

76PP BOOKLET,
LARGE A4 FORMAT, £4,
ISBN 1 903087 72 4

READINGS FROM JAMES

A BOOK OF READINGS BASED ON
THE LIFE OF JAMES

TIM SHENTON

Here is an excellent devotional
for young people and families.
It draws out many lessons to
be learned for everyday life,
and points to Jesus Christ as
the Saviour of the world and
the friend of sinners. Includes
points for thought, prayer, and
memory verse suggestions.

76PP BOOKLET,
LARGE A4 FORMAT, £4,
ISBN 1 903087 61 9

READING YOUR BIBLE

A STARTER'S GUIDE

**GAVIN CHILDRESS
AND AUDREY DOOLEY**

The Bible is the best known
book in the world. Sadly,
although most people have
one at home, it often remains
on the shelf unread. This short
book outlines key details and
facts of each book of the
Bible. Illustrated throughout
with fun pictures and
diagrams.

112PP, PAPERBACK,
ILLUSTRATED, £5.00,
ISBN 1 903087 41 4

LET'S EXPLORE

JOHN G ROBERTS

Written in story form, this illustrated book demonstrates how the Bible speaks to us today by examining a number of topics, starting with each of the Ten Commandments, and moving on to the Lord's Prayer and the Beatitudes. Ideal for parents and Sunday School teachers to use in sharing God's Word with young people.

'…this book deserves a place in every school library.'
OUR INHERITANCE

194PP HARDBACK,
ILLUSTRATED, £5,
ISBN 0 902548 87 5

MY BOOK OF HOBBIES

AND GOD'S BOOK, THE BIBLE

TERENCE PETER CROSBY

In a wide reference to many things, Terence Peter Crosby engages us with pictures of God's wonderful salvation and how to grow in the Christian life.

128PP PAPERBACK,
ILLUSTRATED, £6,
ISBN 1 84625 024 2

SAM AND THE GLASS PALACE

A VICTORIAN ADVENTURE BASED ON THE WORK OF LORD SHAFTESBURY

NORMAN COOK

Sam Clarke was an orphan, forced to run the streets of London, desperately needing an education and, above all, new parents to take care of him. After coming into contact with Lord Shaftesbury, his dream started to come true. But then it started to become a nightmare…

96PP PAPERBACK,
ILLUSTRATED, £5,
ISBN 1 903087 42 0

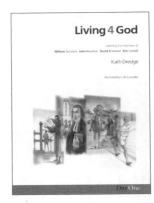

LIVING 4 GOD
TYNDALE, NEWTON, LIDDELL, BRAINERD

KATH DREDGE

A concise book containing biographies of four 'heroes of the faith' to inspire young Christians today: William Tyndale; John Newton; David Brainerd; Olympic athlete Eric Liddell.

'Contains great lessons for us all and is thoroughly recommended.'
GRACE MAGAZINE

72PP BOOKLET,
ILLUSTRATED, £2.00,
ISBN 1 903087 28 7

BIBLE DISCOVER AND COLOUR

ANIMALS, PLANTS, BIRDS AND
PLACES OF THE BIBLE
(FOUR BOOKLETS)

PHILIP SNOW

1 903087 88 0   ANIMALS
1 903087 89 9   BIRDS
1 903087 90 2   PLACES
1 903087 91 0   PLANTS

The pictures in these
colouring books are great fun
for children to colour in, and
each page contains a Bible
quotation as well as some
interesting information on
the places, flora or fauna
illustrated.

32PP EACH, A4 FORMAT
£2.50 EACH OR £9 FOR ALL FOUR

FOOTSTEPS SERIES

FOOTSTEPS OF THE PAST:
JOHN BUNYAN

**ANDREW EDWARDS
AND FLEUR THORNTON**

How a hooligan and soldier
became a preacher, prisoner
and famous writer
32PP LARGE-FORMAT BOOKLET,
ILLUSTRATED, £3
ISBN 1 903087 81 3

FOOTSTEPS OF THE PAST:
WILLIAM BOOTH

**ANDREW EDWARDS
AND FLEUR THORNTON**

The troublesome teenager
who changed the lives of
people no-one else would
touch
32PP LARGE-FORMAT BOOKLET,
ILLUSTRATED, £3
ISBN 1 903087 83 X

FOOTSTEPS OF THE PAST:
WILLIAM CAREY

**ANDREW EDWARDS
AND FLEUR THORNTON**

The shoemaker whose passion
for Jesus brought the Bible
and new life to millions in
India
32PP LARGE-FORMAT BOOKLET,
ILLUSTRATED, £3
ISBN 1 846250 12 9

FOOTSTEPS OF THE PAST:
WILLIAM WILBERFORCE

**ANDREW EDWARDS
AND FLEUR THORNTON**

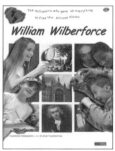

People like Wilberforce relied
totally on God for strength
and courage…. and look
what he managed to achieve!

32PP LARGE-FORMAT BOOKLET,
ILLUSTRATED, £3,
ISBN 1 84625 028 5

Also by Derek Prime

THE LORD'S PRAYER FOR TODAY
DEREK PRIME

The Lord's Prayer is one of the best known passages in the Bible, yet many Christians struggle to enter into the living relationship with God that it endorses. The book applies the prayer to our times and reminds us that only through Christ can we come truly to worship God.

150PP, PAPERBACK, £7,
ISBN 1 903087 56 2

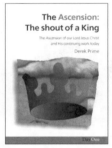

THE ASCENSION: THE SHOUT OF A KING
DEREK PRIME

If we neglect our Saviour's ascension and continuing work, we risk losing sight of his unique and central place in the life of the Church. This book helps to focus us in our spiritual life.

'This book is a winner!'
ENGLISH CHURCHMAN

150PP, PAPERBACK, £5,
ISBN 0 902548 90 5

OPENING UP 1 CORINTHIANS
DEREK PRIME

How should people live in the light of a surrounding immoral culture? What should be the church's response to blatant sin on the part of its members? How should the giving and stewardship of the church be administered? What happens after a person dies? How should spiritual gifts be exercised, and what is the place of love in all this? Here is a succinct treatment of these topics, and an emphasis on the centrality, prominence and glory of the Saviour, the Lord Jesus Christ.

'...a rare combination of sound theological insight and helpful, practical application.'
ALISTAIR BEGG

160PP PAPERBACK, £6,
ISBN 1 84625 004 8

Day One Publications Ryelands Road Leominster Herefordshire HR6 8NZ ☎ 01568 613 740
www.dayone.co.uk **email:** sales@dayone.co.uk